THE PRIMARY LANGUAGE RECORD

Handbook for teachers

CLPE

Centre for Language in Primary Education
Webber Row
London SE1 8QW

This handbook was written by:

Myra Barrs, CLPE
Sue Ellis, CLPE
Hilary Hester, CLPE
Anne Thomas, CLPE

With contributions from:
Helen Kerslake, IBIS, and
Liz Laycock, IBIS
Susanna Steele, Advisory Drama Teacher

Thanks to the following members of CLPE staff for
their help in the production of the handbook:
Doris Anstee
Brenda Hockley,
and to Norris Bentham for her work on the
manuscript.

Design: Maddison/Moore Graphics

Illustrations: Linda Stevens

Photographs: Keith Hawkins, Phil Polglaze, ILEA
Learning Resources Branch, Television and
Publishing Centre

Typesetting: Contemporary Graphics Ltd.
Printed by: Chameleon Press

© Centre for Language in Primary Education

First published in 1988 by CLPE
Reprinted 1988, 1989, 1992, 1995

ISBN 1-872267-00-9

Printed and Bound in the U.K.

Preface

The new Primary Language Record has quite a long history. It began in the Autumn Term of 1985, when a steering group of teachers, head teachers, in-service staff and members of the inspectorate met at the Centre for Language in Primary Education to consider the need for an improved means of recording children's progress in this crucial area of learning. The group discussed existing good practice in the recording of language development, and decided what a new ILEA record would have to take into account. This steering group prepared a brief for a working party which drafted the first version of the record; later a second working party redrafted the record in the light of feedback from users. In the two and a half years that it has taken to develop the record, many people have contributed to the work of the steering group and working parties, and have helped to make the record what it is, and for this I am very grateful.

Possibly the most thorough part of this whole development process was the piloting of the record in 1986-87. More than fifty schools across the ten ILEA divisions agreed to try out the record over a period of two terms and to feed back their responses and suggestions to a coordinating group. The version they tried out was the first draft of the record, and their views and comments informed the work of the second working party which redrafted the record after the pilot phase. This extensive trial process was coordinated by the staff of CLPE and by the Primary IBIS team, all of whom worked alongside teachers in pilot schools to make sure that the final version of the Primary Language Record was as responsive as it could possibly be to the practical needs of teachers in the classroom.

Finally the redrafted Primary Language Record (PLR) was recommended for introduction to all schools by the Education Officer in a report to the Authority in Autumn 1987. While formal consultations still proceed it was decided that the Record should be made available to schools on a voluntary basis from September 1988. There are schools in each Division which have experience of using the PLR, either through participation in the pilot scheme, or in the in-service courses provided by CLPE. These schools will be an important source of expertise in the Division for schools which are beginning to use the PLR.

The Primary Language Record is based on certain principles. In part these reflect the view of record-keeping put forward in the Thomas Report *Improving Primary Schools* (ILEA 1985. para. 2.258). This Report saw three main purposes for record-keeping: to inform and guide other teachers who do not yet know the child; to inform the headteacher and others in positions of responsibility about the child's work; to provide parents with information and assessment of the child's progress. But in addition, the PLR is also based on the principle of the need for records to support and inform the day-to-day teaching in the classroom.

As a consequence certain strands have run through the Primary Language Record from the beginning. They include the involvement of parents – an aspect of the record which was appreciated by parents during the pilot. The record encourages an exchange of information between teachers and parents about a child's language and literacy, and gives a much more detailed and rounded picture of progress than anything provided by the existing record or by a standardised test score alone.

As well as involving parents, the PLR involves children. Teachers in the pilot schools were impressed by children's ability to evaluate their own progress and by the way they responded to the 'Language and Literacy Conference' in particular.

The record also represents a genuine and well thought-out attempt to take account of bilingual development. As far as is currently possible, given the state of our knowledge and our existing resources, the record enables bilingual children's progress and development in their first languages, as well as in English, to be recorded. During the pilot this led to increased cooperation between class teachers and bilingual development/community language teachers.

Last, but definitely not least, the record provides teachers with a framework for teaching language and literacy. Teachers' professional knowledge and their effectiveness are enhanced by careful observation and regular record-keeping. The record, based as it is on some of the best existing practice in ILEA schools, will be helpful for teachers at every stage, from planning to evaluation.

I should like in conclusion to say something about the implications of the Primary Language Record and this accompanying handbook, for school development. The PLR will be introduced through in-service training, and the provision of support materials, for schools who wish to be involved. But, in itself the record also offers, as head teachers and teachers will appreciate, an excellent basis for school-focused in-service meetings and activities. The clear framework of language and literacy development that it provides – based on up-to-date knowledge and on current practice – is a good starting-point for staff discussions, the development of school policies, and for curriculum planning.

In any such discussions, this handbook would be a useful text for 'shared reading' in staff rooms, and it is also a helpful set of guidelines for individual teachers. The handbook underpins the record and provides teachers with ideas and guidance. The idea is not to try and read it in all one go but to use it selectively to help with the completion of the different sections of the record. It constitutes an important ILEA curriculum statement. With the PLR it makes possible a coherent approach across the Authority to language and literacy teaching and learning in the primary school.

I would like to say a personal thank you to all those who have contributed to the development of this new and exciting record. It represents a wealth of experience and knowledge gained over many years and has the potential to ensure children's achievement in this key area of learning so that all children can gain access to the full primary curriculum and in later years to the secondary curriculum.

Barbara MacGilchrist
Senior Staff Inspector, Primary

The Primary Language Record was developed by two working parties and steering committees which met over a period of two and a half years.

Members of the Working Parties

Angela Auset
Gayhurst Infant School
Myra Barrs
Centre for Language in Primary Education
Penny Bentley
Columbia Primary School
Elaine Cain
Mandeville Primary School
Jenny Earlam
Annandale Primary School
Ann Edwards
Primary Reading Adviser, North Thames
Sue Ellis
Centre for Language in Primary Education
David Evans
Sir Thomas Abney Primary School
Denise Halvey
Effra Nursery School
Hilary Hester
Centre for Language in Primary Education
Gulzar Kanji
Staff Inspector (Primary)
Helen Kerslake
Advisory Teacher
Liz Laycock
Centre for Language in Primary Education
Loleta Matthews
Comber Grove Primary School
Moira McKenzie
Centre for Language in Primary Education
Maggie McNeill
Ronald Ross Primary School
Ruby Nelson-Ojo
Advisory Teacher
Nick Oke
Education Psychologist
Gill Palmer
Special Needs Advisory Teacher

Sue Pidgeon
Primary Reading Adviser, South Thames
Kirpal Rihal
Bannockburn Primary School
Helen Savva
Centre for Urban Educational Studies
Anne Thomas
Centre for Language in Primary Education
Anne Vellender
Primary Reading Adviser, South Thames
Lyn Watkins
Inspector (Primary, IBIS)
Silvaine Wiles
Centre for Urban Educational Studies
Margaret Wyeth
Gallions Mount Primary School

Members of the Steering Committees

Alasdair Aston
Acting Staff Inspector (English)
Ann Bostock
Diagnostic Centre for Learning Difficulties
Tony Cline
Principal Educational Psychologist
Ann-Marie Davies
Centre for Urban Educational Studies
Lakshmi de Zoysa
Centre for Urban Educational Studies
Joan Farrelly
Inspector, Special Education
Simon Fuller
English Adviser, Divisions 1 and 10
Barbara MacGilchrist
Senior Staff Inspector (Primary)
Vinnette Melbourne
Inspector (Primary, IBIS)
Leela Ramdeen
Inspector (Multi-ethnic and Anti-racist)
John Stannard
Inspector (Primary)

Members of the Working Parties were also members of the Steering Committees

The PLR was piloted in over fifty ILEA schools in 1986-1987. The schools involved were:

St. Paul's
Sir John Lillie
Miles Coverdale
Bevington
Essendine
St. Dominic's
Eleanor Palmer
Carlton
St. Andrews
Thornhill
Charles Lamb
Woodberry
    Down J.M.
Jubilee
Mandeville
Lauriston
St. Matthias
St. Agnes
Sir William
    Burrough
Stewart Headlam
Annandale
Horn Park I.
Meridian
Bannockburn
Perrymount
Launcelot
Downderry I.
Eliot Bank
Crawford
Michael Faraday
Rotherhithe I.
Rotherhithe J.M.

Effra
Larkhall J.M.
Streatham Wells
Crown Lane
Belleville
Ronald Ross
Penwortham J.M.
Beaver's Holt
James Lee Nursery
Bramber Nursery
Gayhurst I.
John Scurr
Thomas Buxton I.
Gallion's Mount
Woodmansterne
Whitmore
Columbia
Manormead
    Special School
De Beauvoir I.
Harrington Hill
Blue Gate Fields I.
Old Church
    Nursery
Newington Green
    Infant
William Tyndale
Stebon
Aspen House
John Ruskin Language
    Impaired Unit

The pilot was co-ordinated by a central group of CLPE staff and Reading Advisers, together with the Primary IBIS team. The IBIS team members were:

Staff inspector

Gulzar Kanji

Inspectors

Ian Hubbard
Vinnette Melbourne
Britt Parker
Lyn Watkins

Advisory teachers

Gussie Andersen
Julie Bayliss
Hilary Clark
Alvina Harrison
Helen Kerslake
Ruby Nelson-Ojo
Maggie Tarrant
Sally Yates

We acknowledge the help of the following people who read and commented on the handbook:

Barbara MacGilchrist, *SSI Primary*
Gulzar Kanji, *SI Primary*
Joan Farrelly, *Inspector, Special Education*
Kuldip Rai, *Inspector, Bilingual Education*
Ming Tsow, *Inspector, Bilingual Education*

We thank all those schools which have given us permission to use photographs and examples of their records in this handbook.

Contents

Introducing

THE PRIMARY LANGUAGE RECORD

HOW IT WORKS

The Primary Language Record is designed with certain principles in mind:

the involvement of parents

A discussion with the child's parent(s) is the first section of the record form. This section gives parents and teachers the opportunity to meet early in the school year in order to share information and discuss a child's language and literacy development at home and at school. There is also space, in Part C, for parents to comment on the completed record, and to sign the form to indicate that they have read it.

the involvement of children

There are two sections on the record for language/literacy conferences with the child (in the Autumn and Summer Terms). These conferences are intended to provide an opportunity for children to be actively involved in the evaluation of their own progress and the planning of their work.

the involvement of all teachers who teach the child

The record is designed to allow all teachers who teach the child to be involved in compiling a full picture of the child's progress and to ensure that the special insights of bilingual development/community language teachers, support teachers and head teachers are incorporated.

the involvement of children with special educational needs

It is hoped that the approach to language development in the record will be as relevant to teachers in special schools as to those in mainstream schools, and that the observation-based methods of assessment in the record will help teachers of children with special educational needs.

the importance of recording children's progress in the other community languages they know as well as in English

The record offers positive support for the gathering of information about language and literacy developments in languages other than English. This handbook offers a number of ideas as to how such information may be gathered, with the help of bilingual colleagues, or through sensitive observation and questioning. This is an area of rapid development, and many schools will be looking for ways of logging bilingual children's progress in more than one language. It is hoped that the approaches suggested here will be useful to them.

the importance of recording developments across the curriculum in all major language modes

Regular record-keeping is recognised as being an important part of teaching but most official records only ask for brief summative end-of-year statements. The Primary Language Record is accompanied by an optional observation and sample sheet, which allows teachers to make regular, detailed observations of language and literacy development. These observations provide information that teachers can draw on in completing the record.

Developments in language and literacy do not take place in isolation from one another. This record provides a basis for making connections between different aspects of development in all the major language modes – talking and listening, reading, and writing – and for observing children using language for learning across the whole curriculum.

the importance of a clear framework for evaluating progress in language

The record offers a coherent view of what constitutes progress and development in language. It encourages teachers to identify children's strengths and note growth points, to regard errors as information, and to analyse patterns of error in a constructive way. It will be particularly helpful to teachers who are interested in informal methods of assessment, based on observation and on teacher judgement.

The records 'package'

The whole Primary Language Record "package" consists of:

a) the main record – the Primary Language Record – which is an official ILEA record and can replace the language section on the existing yellow/blue record, and

b) an optional observation and sample sheet in four parts, which is intended to help teachers in completing the main record. This observation and sample sheet is a flexible document which can be incorporated into existing record systems and used at teachers' own discretion.

a) The Primary Language Record

The language record (buff form) is designed to be completed at several points in the school year, and not just at the end of the year. In this way it is hoped that it will inform the *teaching* that goes on during the year, and not become merely an administrative record. It should also provide a good basis for discussing a child's progress with parents. Completed records will be passed on throughout the child's primary school career, and into the secondary school, forming a cumulative language profile.

The Record is divided into three parts:

Part A	page 1	to be completed during the Autumn Term
Part B	pages 2 and 3	to be completed during the Spring Term
Part C	page 4	to be completed during the Summer Term (by the Summer half term for 4th year junior children)

At whatever point in the year a child enters school it will be helpful if as much as possible of the record can be filled in, even if some has to remain incomplete.

These timings will obviously vary for some children – for instance, children in the nursery, or those entering school at times of the year other than the beginning of the Autumn Term.

Children in nursery schools or classes may of course be entering the nursery at any point in the school year, and the timings suggested on the record may not therefore be appropriate for them. In these circumstances teachers will obviously need to adapt the suggested timings, and complete as much of the record as seems appropriate, considering the extent of a child's experience in school. However it should always prove valuable to complete part A in a child's first term in the nursery, as the kind of information parents and children can provide about pre-school experiences will help teachers with their planning. Nursery teachers may find that, for children who have four or five terms in the nursery, they need only complete one main record, though they may wish to make fuller use of the observation and sample sheet.

The same considerations will apply to all children entering school at other times of the year than in September, for whatever reason (e.g. family movement, sickness, children in temporary accommodation, children who have had to wait for a place in school). In all cases it will be useful to complete as much of the record as is appropriate, and particularly Part A.

● *Part A consists of:*

a) boxed information of an administrative nature and

b) spaces where the discussion with parents (A1) and the first language/literacy conference with the child (A2) are to be recorded

See pages 10-15 for full notes on the completion of all these sections.

● *Part B 'The Child as a Language User' has sections on*

Talking and listening (B1)
Reading (B2), and
Writing (B3)

Teachers completing Part B may want to draw on the detailed information that they have gained from the observation and sample sheet and/or from their own records. The completed Part B should give a full and balanced picture of the child as a language user.

Each section ends with a space where teachers can record:

a) the experiences and teaching that have helped or would help the child's development in a particular aspect of language, and
b) the outcomes of any discussions that have taken place between the class teacher and the head teacher or the child's parent(s), about the child's development in this aspect of language

Where there is reason for concern about a child's progress or if in any way it is exceptional, it will be useful to arrange such a discussion and record what has been decided.

For further notes on B1, B2 and B3 see pages 16-34.

● *Part C* is designed to allow the information contained in Part B to be added to, so that the account of the child's language progress is as up-to-date as possible. It also provides an opportunity for parents to comment on the record, if they wish to, and for a second language/literacy conference with the child.

For further notes on Part C see page 35.

Observations and Samples (Primary Language Record)

The observation and sample sheet (white form) is a teacher's informal record which complements the Primary Language Record and can be incorporated into a school's own recording systems on an optional basis. The detailed information provided by the observation and sample sheet should be of considerable value to teachers in completing the main Primary Language Record.

The observation and sample sheet is in four parts:
1. Talking and listening: diary of observations
2. Reading and writing: diary of observations
3. Reading samples
4. Writing samples

There is therefore space to record significant developments in language and literacy in an open diary format, and to analyse in depth particular examples of a child's reading and writing. The observation and sample sheet, and the ways in which it might be used as part of teachers' ongoing records, are discussed at more length on pages 36-54. Questions of the organisation and storage of records of this kind are discussed in Appendix A on pages 55-56.

A series of in-service packs focusing on different aspects of language and literacy, for use in school-based in-service meetings, is being planned to accompany the Primary Language Record.

Part A of the Primary Language Record is to be completed during the Autumn Term. It consists of boxed information of an administrative nature, and spaces to record the discussion with parents (A1) and the first language/literacy conference with the child (A2).

The following notes may be of help to teachers completing the information section.

Summer-Born

The term 'summer-born' refers to those children with birthdays occurring between May and August (inclusive). Reports seem to indicate that some summer-born children are at a disadvantage where they have had less experience of school than their peers because of being so much younger.

An awareness of this as a possible factor in children's language and learning development is important, although care should also be taken to avoid having lower expectations for children who are summer-born.

Language(s) understood, language(s) spoken, language(s) read, language(s) written

For many children in the class 'English' may be the only language recorded here. But for bilingual children there may be several entries. Many children will know English and another language or languages.

Distinctions are made between understanding, speaking, reading and writing because of some children's wide linguistic experiences. For example a child may speak, read and write a home/community language and English, and be further literate in a third language such as Arabic for reading the Qu'ran; a child may speak Panjabi, and write Urdu.

Children themselves may be able to give the information needed for this box, but you will need to be sensitive to children's feelings when talking about their use of languages apart from English. Some children may not know the names of the languages, or offer what they think adults will understand (e.g. 'Indian' or 'Pakistani'), or they may have reservations about revealing their linguistic background. These questions from the Linguistic Minorities Project survey may be helpful: 'Do you speak any languages at home other than English?' 'What is the name of that

▶ D   *1st year juniors-boy*
    Languages: English

This is part A of D's record. Parts B and C appear on pages 16-17 and page 35.

Primary Language Record

School	School Year
	86 87

Name: D

DoB: 28 3 79
☑ Boy ☐ Girl

Summer born child ☐

Languages understood: English
Languages spoken: English

Languages read: English
Languages written: English.

Details of any aspects of hearing, vision or coordination affecting the child's language/literacy. Give the source and date of this information.

Names of staff involved with child's language and literacy development

Class teacher.

Part A   To be completed during the Autumn Term

A1 Record of discussion between child's parent(s) and class teacher

Chooses to read at home often prompted by his older sister's enthusiasm for reading. All sorts of books - stories, poems, comics, picks out words from newspapers to read and write. Makes up stories, asks for words for ideas or uses his own ideas (mostly) Ghost stories and monster stories are favoured. Tries spellings but asks if stuck. Attempts to use dictionary. Inquisitive mind, always asks what words mean. Watches television. Good visual memory, good observations. Impatient if finds work too hard though willing. Wants to achieve but sometimes lacks concentration in reading and writing.

Signed: Parent(s) _____   Teacher _____

Date _____

A2 Record of language/literary conference with child

"What Is A Ghost Going To Do" is D's favourite book. "I like to be able to read so I can read stories to my sister, I sometimes make up stories to tell her. I'm not that good a reader 'cos sometimes I forget the words, I don't know them. I ask my sister and she gives me a clue. I read at home every night." Given the choice D would watch television rather than read. "I make up ghost stories and copy from books - my mum helps with spellings. My best bit of writing was when I wrote about the tele. programme Dungeons and Dragons. Sometimes I'm a bit lazy with handwriting and I chat too much, but sometimes it's okay."

Date _____

©ILEA 1988

language?' 'Can you write that language?'. For young children, their parent(s) and parents' friends, older sisters and brothers, or colleagues in school who know children's languages will be able to help fill in this box. And the discussion with parents as the starting point for these records will give a fuller picture of the child's language and literacy experiences in languages apart from English.

For a fuller discussion of languages bilingual children understand, speak, read and write, see Appendix B.

Details of any aspects of hearing, vision or coordination affecting the child's language/literacy

This section provides an opportunity to note anything about a child's hearing, vision or physical coordination that is significantly affecting

the child's learning and participation in the work of the classroom. Please record only recent evidence, substantiated by medical or specialist investigation. Teachers should quote the source of information and when it was gathered. This is important as the nature or severity of a difficulty may change over time. All quotations must be from open files and not from confidential medical records.

Teachers may notice in the classroom what they think might be signs of physical or sensory difficulty (e.g. hearing/visual impairment) which might be affecting the development of the child's language or literacy. They should check with the open school record and with previous teachers. If they are concerned, they should also consult with the headteacher and with the child's parent(s). The parent(s) may be able to help a teacher to understand what s/he observes in the light of their experience and knowledge of their child, or inform her/him about anything they have noticed

at home. With the parents' permission, the school doctor or nurse may be able to provide more information, from records or from further investigation, if this seems appropriate. Otherwise all medical records (including, for example, the results of hearing tests) are confidential.

When completing Part B of the record, this note can be referred to and the teacher can describe how s/he and the child together have dealt with the difficulty, in the context of the development of the child's language and literacy at school. Have any ways of working been found that are particularly supportive for the child in class? In what social settings do these take place? Is the child developing any ways of communicating, reading or recording that are useful in getting round the difficulty, or diminishing it? Whilst bearing children's physical difficulties in mind when completing all parts of the record, teachers should focus on what children *can* do. This can then provide a positive basis for further work by parents and other teachers.

List of staff involved with child's language and literacy development:

Name all the members of staff who are working with the child, including, where appropriate, the child's community school teachers. Say in what way each one is involved.

For example:
(Name) – classroom teacher
(Name) – bilingual development/community
language teacher at school
(Name) – community language teacher outside
school
(Name) – support teacher
(Name) – section 11 teacher
(Name) – nursery nurse
(Name) – head teacher

In some cases (especially in the nursery) it will be appropriate to include support staff in this list. Nursery nurses will often be involved in the recording of children's language development and may be adding their observations to the observation and sample sheet.

A1 Record of discussion between child's parent(s) and class teacher

N.B. 'Parent' in this form will also include a person 'in loco parentis'.

The purpose of the discussion between parent(s) and teacher is to encourage a two-way communication between home and school, to let parent(s) share their knowledge of the child, at home and at school, their observations and concerns, hopes and expectations. Regular informal conversations between parents and teachers can help to establish a real partnership between home and school and can create a forum where achievements as well as concerns can be discussed. The teacher will be able to respond to these in the child's record over the year, and discuss the child's development again at the end of the year. Research into home/school reading links shows that children's learning at home has an important influence on learning at school.

development teacher or a community interpreter would help. Teachers should be aware, of course, of the constraints which arise when one parent is 'interviewed' by two people. Where possible, the teacher who speaks the same language as the parent(s) should organise the discussion.

– it should be made clear from the outset that the child is the centre of the discussion, and that the purpose of the discussion is to enable the parents to contribute to the child's language record. The teacher's role in the discussion is primarily to listen to what the parent has to say and to ensure that a fair record is made of the discussion.

– consider questions such as: who should write on the form? Should it always be the teacher? How can parents have equal access to the form during the discussion? Should notes be taken in the course of the discussion – or might it be

Procedure

The organisation of this discussion is left to the discretion of the school. It is envisaged that, some time in the first term, there will be an informal discussion of about 15 minutes between parent(s) and teacher. Some parents (and teachers) may find the interview intimidating and it is important that it is not seen as a formal interview but as a means of sharing knowledge.

The way the discussion is arranged will affect the quality of the content of the conversation between the parent(s) and teacher:

– if possible invite the parents directly, through a phone call, letter, or conversation. Where appropriate, letters home will need to be translated. Many schools will already have introduced the idea of the discussion through letters to parents, through meetings at parents' evenings, or through informal contact.

– try to arrange a time that is mutually convenient, and to keep to any agreed time-limit in discussion (some parents may have taken time off work, or made child-care arrangements to visit the school). Many schools will use the appointments systems already established on parents' evenings to arrange the discussion with parents.

– try to offer as comfortable and private a space as possible for the discussion to take place, so that the situation is welcoming, relaxed, and friendly. Think carefully about seating and ensure that parents are not put at a disadvantage in any way.

– where parents are not experienced in using English, suggest that someone who could interpret is invited – parents could bring friends, relative, or older siblings, or perhaps a bilingual

---

A1 Record of discussion between child's parent(s) and class teacher

M. loves her reading book that she takes home. She is very active and always involved in something. She is now settled at bedtime by listening to a story tape. M. likes TV and knows many songs and rhymes. She talks a great deal about the books and rhymes she knows from nursery.

Signed: Parent(s) _____   Class Teacher _____

Date _____

▲ [M] *Nursery — girl*
Languages: **English**

▼ [R] *Top infant — boy*
Languages: **English**

A1 Record of discussion between child's parent(s) and class teacher

At home when the T.V is on R. is selective with his viewing. Cities of Gold is a favourite. He plays lots of imaginary games, with soft toys and teddy bears. He enjoys lego modelling. He is not interested in board games at the minute. He helps drying up in the kitchen. He likes going to the chute with the rubbish. He never stops talking and asks a lot of questions. Sometimes he writes, draws and colours. He does things in phases. He is always reading. He likes a bed time story. He reads PACT books and others.

Signed: Parent(s) _____   Class Teacher _____

Date _____

better to agree on a summary and record the discussion at the end? Should the record of the discussion always be only in English?

At the end of this discussion teacher and parent(s) should agree the points to be recorded on the Record. This summary will become part of the open record, but the *detail* of the discussion between parent and teacher is confidential.

Starting points for discussion – some suggestions

The discussion gives parents the opportunity to comment on the children's reading, writing and talk at home. It should be made clear that this kind of information from home will be a great help to the teacher, and will give a fuller picture of the child's development in language.

Some families may use more than one language

at home and knowledge about a child's talk, reading and writing in a first language adds an important dimension to the teacher's understanding of the child as a language user. It may sometimes be necessary to talk to parents about the ways in which the school encourages bilingual children to use their first language(s) and the reasons for doing so, for example, the fact that it provides continuity between home and school and that children can draw on what they know about their first language(s) for their learning in English.

Some of the topics that could be discussed:
– the child's knowledge and enjoyment of story and opportunities that might be possible for story telling and story listening.
– some of the child's favourite stories and rhymes.
– the kinds of reading the child enjoys at home e.g. comics, their own books, books from school. With young children, evidence that they are aware of the print around them e.g. on T.V., signs, computers, etc; whether the child chooses to read.
– what parents have observed about children's use of language(s) at home.
– whether or not there are community schools in the area which the child does or could attend.
– opportunities that might be possible for writing at home and whether the child chooses to write.
– the child's special interests at home, including favourite toys, games, T.V. programmes.
– changes that parents have observed in children's language and literacy development and any concerns they might have.

From time to time the teacher may need to guide the conversation. Some useful ways of doing this might be:
– referring to parents' observations on the previous record
– using open-ended questions, e.g. "tell me about . . ." or, "what do you think about . . ."
– contributing one's own observations
– inviting parents to say more about a particular point.

It is important to remember that this is a conversation between parent(s) and teacher. It gives an opportunity both for parents to say what their own priorities are for children, and for observations to be shared.

> These examples of discussions between parents and teachers help us to realise how much children know and how much they are involved in a range of language and literacy-related activities at home and in the community. We are told of the important influences on children's development at home, interaction with brothers and sisters, television viewing, likes and dislikes, and are shown evidence of bilingual children's development in their first languages. Knowledge of this kind can inform subsequent teaching.

A1 Record of discussion between child's parent(s) and class teacher

O. is very interested in reading information books especially the Ladybird series. The science ones are his main choice. He's not easily distracted by his younger brother and sister when he's engrossed in his books. He also enjoys cutting and sticking pictures. He likes to look in his older sister's books. He can speak Ibo, a Nigerian language – used preferably when putting his six year old brother in his place.

Signed: Parent(s) _____ Class Teacher _____

Date _____

▲ [O] **2nd year junior — boy**
Languages: **English, Ibo**

▼ [P] **Special school — 10 year old — boy**
Languages: **English**

A1 Record of discussion between child's parent(s) and class teacher

P. loves books, particularly about ships, planes and any other vehicles. Dad spends time with P. who repeats what he has read. Mum also spends time with him and P. translates the pictures. He loves telling stories. He is very keen on Transformers, he likes to draw them, knows all their names + whether they are good or bad. He enjoys Transformer magazines and comics. P. is keen to visit places and can pick out names like Police Station and fire engine etc. He also loves shopping and is very good at picking out the names on various items. He enjoys T.V. + plays at speech from some programmes and dances to the music. Enjoys imaginative play using mops for guns etc. P. is very tidy-minded and likes to help his mum around the house. Speech is continuing to develop, much clearer than it used to be.

Signed: Parent(s) _____ Class Teacher _____

Date _____

A2 Language and literacy conference – child and the teacher

Purpose

A language and literacy conference is designed to give the child an opportunity to talk about and discuss with the teacher her/his experiences, achievements and interests as a language user. A conference like this should be a continuation of an already existing dialogue between child and teacher, and a means of establishing, in a more structured way, children's views of themselves as language learners and language users in and outside school. It should also encourage the child to play an increasingly active part in her/his own learning and provide regular opportunities to reflect on progress.

The conference can provide a formal opportunity for the child and teacher to develop their joint working relationship. It can also enable the teacher to:

- listen to the child's views and gain an understanding of her/his language experiences in and outside school.

- use this information to describe the development and learning that is taking place.

- give positive feedback.

- find out about any concerns.

- discuss and help the child to formulate positive strategies to use in her/his learning.

- extend the range and variety of literacy experiences (which would include the child's own choices).

- record decisions arrived at during the conference.

Timing

It is suggested in the Primary Language Record that at least two conferences should take place each year: one of these would be in the Autumn Term (A2) and another in the Summer Term (C2).

Suggested procedure

The child would be asked to bring to the conference a self-chosen selection of books or other texts in English and/or other community languages that s/he had read recently, and a selection of her/his writing, which might include writing in more than one language.

In the case of a bilingual child a bilingual development/community language teacher would naturally be involved in these conferences, if at all possible. The child would feel more able to share

thoughts and feelings about her/his community language – spoken and written – with a fluent speaker-reader-writer. This teacher and the class teacher might divide the responsibility for the conference, and the conference time, between them.

The setting for each conference should be as informal as possible. It is important that the child should feel at ease and able to talk freely about work and concerns. As far as possible the conferences should become a normal part of classroom practice.

The child would be invited to talk about her/himself as a reader, writer, and a language user both in and outside school. It would be important to discover what the child saw as important elements in her/his language and literacy developments, and to allow time for discussing interests, reviewing progress, and establishing the child's own perceptions of her/his strengths and weaknesses.

Open-ended questions would enable the child to say what s/he thinks and feels about her/his achievements, concerns, and areas of

---

A2 Record of language/literacy conference with child

(often chooses Bengali books) "I like Bengali reading" "In Bangladesh I did read books, that's why I like. I'm better at Bengali reading" (English books) "Sometimes I understand, sometimes I don't understand." If he can't read a word he says he asks somebody else, or leaves it out. (At home) "I'm reading and writing Bengali and English." Looking at his Bengali writing he told me a bit of that story. "I like it." He thinks he should talk English more to improve it.

Date _____

▲ [S] *4th year junior — boy*
Languages: **Bengali, English, Arabic (Koran)**

A2 Record of language/literacy conference with child

'I like writing and stories are my favourite. I've got those sort (Read it Yourself) of books at home. I don't read them to Becky, she doesn't listen.' Li. sees herself as a writer and enjoys illustrating her detailed stories. She likes reading at home and in school – if it's quiet! She contributes to group and one to one discussions readily but she seldom chats in class discussions as 'everyone's always calling out before I've thought.' Li. enjoys writing more than anything else at school except playtimes.'

Date _____

▲ Li *1st year junior — girl*
Languages: English

A2 Record of language/literacy conference with child

L. loves reading and her favourite books are 'The Snowman' and 'The 3 Bears'. L. thinks she is quite good at reading. She uses the pictures to help know what the print says and asks a grown up to read to her if she can't read the book on her own. L. can get better at reading by looking at the words and letters (she sounded out a word) L. enjoys writing more at home than at school because her mum helps. She likes writing "a little bit." Writing is useful for writing books, letters, about your models and shopping lists, otherwise it would be like 'Don't Forget the Bacon!"

Date _____

▲ L *Middle-infant — girl*
Languages: English

A2 Record of language/literacy conference with child

A's favourite book is 'Superfudge' although she enjoys all Judy Blume books, "because they are realistic." They are about how children get on with their parents. She also likes poetry books, particularly if they are funny. "They give you a break from long stories." At home A. reads her mum's history books. She likes reading stories and says she reads in bed, or if there's nothing on the T.V. She thinks her reading is gradually improving because she can "pronounce words better now." She likes writing stories and thinks her writing is improving.

Date _____

▲ A *4th year junior — girl*
Languages: English

improvement in language and literacy. Once children were at ease in the conference, they would feel free to initiate more, and to participate more fully. Most children really appreciate the chance to give their own views and discuss their progress in this way, and the summarising of the conference on the record itself is an important indication that what they say is being taken seriously.

Very often as children grow older they become more private. They may like to keep separate some of their outside interests and teachers would respect their feelings. On the other hand, it often needs to be made clear to children that interests which exist beyond the confines of school are not only relevant and valid in themselves, but of great interest in discussions about their language/literacy development. So it will be positively useful to invite discussion of T.V. viewing, experiences of story, hobbies and leisure reading, including comics and magazines.

◀ *These examples of conferences give a clear impression of children evaluating their own work and reflecting on their progress. They show children's preferences for different styles of working and working contexts, and allow children to make links between literacy at home and at school. Where teachers have quoted directly there is a strong sense of the child's voice.*

These conferences allow teachers of bilingual children to gain an insight into the way that both their languages are developing and supporting their learning. In general the conferences have provided children with the opportunity to reflect on their favourite activities, choices of books and their reasons for making particular choices, and enabled them to play a greater part in their own learning.

B

The organisation of this section

Part B is the second phase of the Primary Language Record (PLR), and should be completed during the Spring Term. From the beginning of the year detailed notes will have been made in teachers' own day-to-day records and/or on the observation and sample sheet about aspects of the child's progress in talking/listening, reading and writing. These notes can be drawn on when filling in Part B.

Part B is divided into three sections: B1 Talking and listening; B2 Reading; B3 Writing. There is space for making two kinds of entry in each section.

First, observations on the child's progress in that aspect of language development.

Second, a brief description of any experiences or teaching that has supported (or could support) the child's development, and which would be useful information for the receiving teacher(s). If the child's progress has been giving concern or is in any way exceptional this is also the place to record the outcomes of any formal discussion with other members of staff, with parents or with outside agencies such as the Schools Psychological Service.

Once Part B has been completed it will need to be signed by the head teacher because s/he has overall responsiblity for the child's progress. It should also be signed by any other teacher(s) who have contributed to the entries for each section – such as the bilingual development/community language teacher, the Section 11 teacher, or other support staff.

Relationships between the sections

Although separated here, the aspects of language to be monitored – talking and listening, reading and writing – are all interrelated. Often developments in one area will mirror or support development in another. For example, books children read will influence their spoken and written language – introducing them to new styles of use as well as to new words. And talking together about work they are doing or books they are reading will deepen children's understanding of concepts and ideas they are exploring. The double page spread of Part B reflects this close relationship between each of the three sections and should make it possible to see at a glance a child's development in each area.

▶ *The continuation of D's record from page 10. Part C appears on page 35.*

Part B
To be completed during the Spring Term and to include information from all teachers currently teaching the child

Child as a language user (one or more languages)
Teachers should bear in mind the Authority's Equal Opportunities Policies (race, gender and class) in completing each section of the record and should refer to *Educational Opportunities for All?*, the ILEA report on special educational needs.

B1 Talking and listening
Please comment on the child's development and use of spoken language in different social and curriculum contexts, in English and/or other community languages: evidence of talk for learning and thinking; range and variety of talk for particular purposes; experience and confidence in talking and listening with different people in different settings.

D. Enjoys talking in class (to the class) and usually has an interesting experience to relate about most subjects under discussion! Loves drama and will happily take on any role in an extrovert fashion. He is interested in other children's opinions and experiences and he is a good listener – even though he sometimes does not appear to be paying attention.

What experiences and teaching have helped/would help development in this area? Record outcomes of any discussion with head teacher, other staff, or parent(s).

Opportunities to be made for him to work in a small group, in an activity which involves discussion and 'presenting' conclusions to other groups or the class.

B2 Reading
Please comment on the child's progress and development as a reader in English and/or other community languages: the stage at which the child is operating (refer to the reading scales on pages 26-27); the range, quantity and variety of reading in all areas of the curriculum; the child's pleasure and involvement in story and reading, alone or with others; the range of strategies used when reading and the child's ability to reflect critically on what is read.

D. is quiet and hesitant when reading aloud, more confident when reading silently – tackling known and predictable texts. He has an obvious awareness of the structure of language. Read 'who not' for 'oh no', relating 'oh' to a word he knew. Using syntactic, grapho-phonic and semantic cues.

continued

B2 (cont)

Enjoys reading and has a firm view of what he does or does not want to read. At the moment I would describe him as a non-fluent reader on reading scale 1.

What experiences and teaching have helped/would help development in this area? Record outcomes of any discussion with head teacher, other staff, or parent(s).

I think D. could be encouraged to be more aware of the idea of reading for pleasure and that he would benefit from a lot of shared reading experiences. I will make sure he has a wide variety of reading material to choose from.

B3 Writing
Please comment on the child's progress and development as a writer in English and/or other community languages: the degree of confidence and independence as a writer; the range, quantity and variety of writing in all areas of the curriculum; the child's pleasure and involvement in writing both narrative and non-narrative, alone and in collaboration with others; the influence of reading on the child's writing; growing understanding of written language, its conventions and spelling.

D. has explored many forms of writing including own stories, retelling stories, letter writing, factual and informative work. He is able to identify some of his spelling mistakes. He enjoys story writing very much. He is aware of the conventions of written language and uses capital letters and full-stops accurately. His writing is lively and expresses interesting ideas.

What experiences and teaching have helped/would help development in this area? Record outcomes of any discussion with head teacher, other staff, or parent(s).

If D. does not have an audience in mind or a purpose for his writing then he works with little enthusiasm. He enjoys reading his finished work aloud to his chosen audience. Re-drafting is useful for D. as his concern for spelling and punctuation are time-consuming and can curb his enthusiasm.

Signature of head teacher and all teachers contributing to this section of the record:

Head teacher

Parent
Class teacher

Child as a language user (one or more languages)

This record is designed to enable teachers to log the progress of all children in the class. Developments in bilingual children's first languages should also be recorded on the PLR, giving as full a picture as possible of the range of languages and dialects that a child uses, or is learning to use. Observations of children and examples of their work should reflect their bilingualism. Teachers who share the same first languages as their bilingual children will be at an obvious advantage here. Teachers who speak only English (or only one or two of the languages spoken by children in their class) will need to seek the help of colleagues who are bilingual in other languages – teachers who work in the same school, or in the community schools that children may attend. Children themselves may readily give information about which language(s) they use most confidently.

Where none of this is possible teachers should look for some of the signs that can give some indication of the child's competence in the first language and their confidence in using it in the school setting. These will include: switching from talking in one language to another as the situation demands; clearly reading with some fluency a text that the teacher may not herself be able to understand; writing in the first language (e.g. when taking notes). At the discussion with parents, parents may also be willing to discuss languages children speak and read in the home setting, although as the notes for the parent conference explain, parents may sometimes have reservations about doing this.

The learning environment

In thinking about the classroom context for language and learning, it is important to include both social and curriculum dimensions.

The social context in which children learn can have a crucial effect on their performance in school.

Children benefit from the experience of working in a variety of different groups and forming learning relationships with other children and with adults, e.g. working with a partner, collaborating in small groups, participating in a whole-class presentation, discussing a piece of work with an adult, reading with a younger/older child.

The curriculum context should provide children with opportunities to contribute the linguistic experience, knowledge and understanding they bring to school and to extend these through a range of classroom activities and materials.

For this to happen, children need to see their culture(s) and language(s) accurately reflected in the books and resources they encounter across the curriculum, as well as to meet worlds that lie beyond their immediate experience.

When choosing and developing themes and topics it is important to ensure that they are accessible to all children, e.g. in a class exploring the theme 'travel', experiences ranging from 'planning a school visit' to 'settling in a new country' can be shared and developed. The way a theme is approached, structured and resourced determines the relevance and meaning it has for the community of children in the class and therefore affects the learning opportunities it offers.

If either the curriculum or the organisation is inadequate, then children's learning will not receive the kind of support it needs: a child's progress or lack of progress should always be seen in relation to the adequacy of the context provided.

The learning environment and equal opportunities

This all becomes more significant in an Authority such as ILEA which has a strong commitment to promoting equal opportunities for all children. Resourcing and organisation need to be planned within the frameworks for thinking about race, gender and class provided both in schools' own equal opportunities policies and the Authority's guidelines. Some of the practical implications of this for the teacher in the classroom will be:

- choosing books and materials that recognise and value children's cultures, lives and experiences

- providing books in languages that children speak – both dual language texts and texts in languages other than English

- recognising material that is biased or tokenist in content and presentation (e.g. the portrayal of gender roles) and which is based on outdated or prejudiced views of people and communities in other areas of the world

- teaching children to respond critically to materials, books and the media, and to explore the intention of authors of books and makers of programmes

– organising learning groups and resources to match and extend children's developing use of language

The connections between race, class, gender and children's progress have been well documented. In addressing the issues of gender and learning, teachers can develop strategies which positively affect the language and literacy development of both girls and boys. By recognising, for example, that girls may do less well working with boys than with other girls, a teacher can create opportunities for them to work in all-female groups for some activities. Boys can be encouraged to practise as listeners and to participate in discussion with an awareness of the views and needs of other members of the group, perhaps through evaluating a tape-recording of their discussion. In acknowledging that boys often do less well with reading in the primary school than girls, particular thought can be given to developing their interest in books, by extending the range of resources available or by trying different approaches, for example encouraging children to make tape-recordings of favourite stories and poems for the school/class library.

Similarly, positive steps can be taken to structure situations in which children use their community language or home dialect for learning in the classroom. An atmosphere needs to be established in which language variety is prominent and encouraged, e.g. providing opportunities for children to work in shared-language groups, offering children the choice of the language they write in, providing materials with examples of different dialect forms....

These and other implications are discussed more fully in the sections that follow, and in the INSET packs that will accompany this Handbook. However it is worth noting two other ideas here.

First, children and adults bring with them into the classroom the attitudes of the world outside. If children experience antipathy because of ethnic origin it will crucially affect their view of themselves as learners. Secondly some children will have experienced hostility to their colour or their language. They (and their families) will need reassuring that the school welcomes them and will provide them with opportunities that they need in order to succeed. Children, for example, may be unwilling to reveal that they speak or read another language if they know that such revelations invite the ridicule of their peers. In the long term a school's equal opportunities policy will need to permeate the whole of the curriculum and school organisation if children are to make progress in their learning.

The learning environment and children with special educational needs in the mainstream classroom

The needs of children with learning difficulties both in mainstream schools and in special education should be given particular consideration. Children with special needs should, like all children, have access to a broad curriculum. This has implications for the selection of resources and for developing ways of working that support children's learning and enable them to play an active role in the classroom.

For children with physical disabilities there are additional implications for the organisation of the classroom and for curriculum planning to ensure that they have equal opportunities for learning.

It is important to remember that the rate at which the children learn will vary, and will also depend on the activity and the demands it makes on them. Some children may require more time for learning than others, for example they may need more opportunities for exploring the meaning in a particular story than their peers.

Children also have different learning styles and, particularly for children with special needs, it is important to find the different ways in which they can gain access to ideas. In carrying out a science investigation, for example, they may be invited to discuss their findings in small groups, make a list of the questions they raise, represent their information in the form of a diagram or write it down in pairs, perhaps as a zig-zag book. There are also implications here for considering the ways children interact with each other, and the social contexts in which individuals are able to contribute, and for the structuring of groups.

The nature of the support they are given, the timing, degree, and the nature of intervention by staff, is crucial to children's development from dependence to independence.

Talking with parents and colleagues is often valuable for finding ways of meeting individual children's needs. A sharing of information may lead to jointly developed strategies e.g. home-school partnerships to support a child's reading.

Following discussion with the head-teacher, it may be decided to involve a support agency, for example, a special needs teacher, to collaborate with the class teacher in providing support for the child. This should be noted and parents kept informed of concerns regarding a child's language and literacy development and the outcomes of any intervention.

B1 Talking and listening

Like sections B2 and B3, Reading and Writing, this section is to be filled in during the Spring Term (or with Nursery-age children during the second term of school — see page 9). This is the place for teachers to look back to their classroom records of a child's use of spoken language — including the Talking and listening diary of observations — and to draw conclusions about the child's development as a communicator up to this point in the year. Further observations about the child's progress after the Spring Term can be added later in Part C.

Observing talk and listening

Keeping a record of children's development in talking and listening may present difficulties not found when recording children's development as readers and writers. First there is no tangible 'product' from which to draw conclusions such as a piece of writing or a book – talk disappears into the air. (It is possible to make a 'product' by tape-recording a child or group of children as they work and talk together, although sometimes this is not feasible.)

Second, the teacher is often *part* of the interaction that is being observed, and holds the dual role of being a contributor to and, at the same time, the monitor of a discussion. This is made more complex in many ILEA classrooms where children will be using their community languages as well as English. Few teachers understand all the languages heard in their classrooms, although children's development in their first languages will play a central role in their overall language development.

In spite of these possible difficulties, it is worth remembering that:

– teachers are observing and listening to children all the time as they work and talk in the classroom. Most of these informal observations are held in the memory. This section and the 'Talking and listening: diary of observations' offer a way of recording and making them permanent.

– teachers most skilled at doing this are often teachers of young children for whom children's development as talkers and the role of talk in learning has traditionally been important. And such skills can be developed over a period of time.

– in many schools there are class teachers and visiting teachers who do speak some of the community (other than English) languages of their children, and their advice can be sought: some schools also have links with teachers in community schools; parents in discussion with their child's teacher will also be able to offer their insights and observations.

– most observations of children's talk can be made informally while working with children individually or in small groups, or, by listening to children as they work in pairs or small groups on their own. It will be enough to note afterwards what seemed significant, with some details of the context for it. Occasionally it may be helpful to set up a special situation and to tape-record children at work, in order to make a more detailed analysis of their talking. This is always a valuable exercise, for it can yield very useful information both about particular children's skills and about the dynamics of talk, and it will inform all subsequent observations.

Social and cognitive dimensions of talk

It is helpful to keep in mind that there are two main dimensions of talk – a social dimension and a cognitive dimension. The matrix on the observation and sample sheets shows these distinctions and suggests a way of mapping the interaction between them. For above all else talk is about interaction. It is to do with *interaction between people*. It is the principal means of making contact with others, and building relationships. It is also to do with *interaction between ideas* – children hear new ideas, put forward new ideas, and develop new ideas through talking with others.

This complex interplay between the social and the cognitive makes the analysis of children's talk and of their spoken language development a demanding task. Is one looking at a child's language, understanding of ideas, or social skills? Action to promote children's development will need to take into account the three dimensions. It will be important to think about ways of supporting a child's confidence in group situations (the size of the group, the members of the group); to analyse any activity for the opportunities it offers chidren for using and extending their language and to anticipate the cognitive demands it will make on them. It will be equally important to decide how any activity can be organised so that talking and listening are necessary.

Since language, learning and social interaction are so closely related and interlinked, they lie at the heart of teaching and learning in the primary classroom. If children are to develop their skills at talking and listening, classrooms and learning contexts need to be organised in such a way that children have opportunities for doing so.

B1 Talking and listening
Please comment on the child's development and use of spoken language in different social and curriculum contexts, in English and/or other community languages: evidence of talk for learning and thinking; range and variety of talk for particular purposes; experience and confidence in talking and listening with different people in different settings.

When CW started school he was very quiet and withdrawn, avoiding confrontation with other children. He said nothing, and nodded his head in response to questions in English. If encouraged he would repeat "Yes" or "No". He goes around all the time with another Chinese boy, CL, who is much more outgoing. He would mimic him and follow his lead. He would look to see what CL did or said before responding, even with choosing food at dinnertime.

Over the last half term something has begun to click. He really has come on. He is much more verbal and adventurous. He now strays from CL's side at times and speaks more for himself. He will come up to you and volunteer information or show you things. 'Look, I got a car.' 'Tricia, I had that first – I play. I found it.' "My sister got me of these at home."

However he is still happiest with his special friend or in a small group. He is noticeably beginning to enjoy being at school.

What experiences and teaching have helped/would help development in this area? Record outcomes of any discussion with head teacher, other staff, or parents.

◀ **CW** *Nursery — boy*
*Languages: **Cantonese, English***

This extract gives a clear picture of CW's early adjustment both to school and to learning through a new language. It is a period for him of watching other children and listening carefully to them, supported by his friendship with a boy who shares the same first language. He responds initially in non-verbal ways to questions in English, then ventures one-word answers and often echoes what his friend says. Finally, with growing confidence in the new context, he begins to talk in English about things important to him. He still feels more secure in the small group with his friend. (see also the first example on page 37)

B1 Talking and listening
Please comment on the child's development and use of spoken language in different social and curriculum contexts, in English and/or other community languages: evidence of talk for learning and thinking; range and variety of talk for particular purposes; experience and confidence in talking and listening with different people in different settings.

> S's confidence as a talker has developed so much since I first knew her. Through her conversations with me and her contribution to class discussions it is possible to sense that S. thinks quite carefully before she speaks, and when she has formed an opinion or judgement she will stick to it. She is quite happy to ask me to explain any difficulties she may be having, though at one time she would not dream of doing this.

What experiences and teaching have helped/would help development in this area? Record outcomes of any discussion with head teacher, other staff, or parents.

> Experience of working with any children in small collaborative work — she tends to stick to the same people.....

Growth and development

In thinking about growth and development in spoken language, it is crucial to make a distinction between children's *knowledge of the system* of the language, and the *uses and purposes* they have for it, even though in reality they cannot be separated – for through *using* language children's *knowledge* of it grows. The distinction makes it possible to think both about children's growing control over the language and the expanding range of purposes they are using it for.

By the age of five the majority of children have learned to use the main structural features of their language, its sound system and much vocabulary. Most of the research in children's spoken language development has focused on those early years of acquisition and there has been little research on later development.

However it is clear that children's vocabularly continues to expand as they meet new concepts and new contexts: they learn new words, and known words and combinations of words acquire new and metaphorical meanings. Also they use structural features of the language in more complex ways, and for expressing more subtle shades of meaning. Models for doing this will come both from interacting with more experienced users of the language (adults and older children) and from stories and poems they hear and read.

In addition to this *knowledge of the system* of the language, by the age of five the majority of

▶ **Sh** **Top junior — girl**
Languages: *Sylheti, Bengali, English*

A powerful picture of a child in her fourth year in the Junior school, moving confidently between her 'first' and second languages. Her appreciation of punning provides evidence of her deepening understanding of the English language. She is supportive of children less experienced at using English than she is, and understands how to help them.

◀ **S** **Top infant — girl**
Languages: *English*

These observations show S's growing social confidence in talking with her teacher and participating in class discussions. She is a child who reflects carefully before making a contribution. From her observations, the teacher realises that S. needs wider experience of working in small groups sometimes with children she knows less well.

children are skilled *users* of the language, and understand many of the social dimensions of talk: they initiate conversations, they ask and respond to questions, they develop conversations and monitor what is being said, and they appreciate the essential turn-taking nature of talk. Often a child's skill as a participant in discussions will be evidenced as much through listening as through talking.

For bilingual children these two strands will be developing through home/community languages as well as through English. They will be skilled users of the 'first' language (for some bilingual children this may be English), and will bring their skills with them to the learning of the second language. What will be new for them will be the system of the new language, but they will be able to use their understanding of the social dimension, learned for the first language. In learning to use a second language children generally move through developmental phases that mirror those they passed through in learning a first language.

However, they will have a wider range of strategies to draw on in learning the second language, because they will already have a knowledge of one language system, and will be comparing and contrasting what they know with

B1 Talking and listening
Please comment on the child's development and use of spoken language in different social and curriculum contexts, in English and/or other community languages: evidence of talk for learning and thinking; range and variety of talk for particular purposes; experience and confidence in talking and listening with different people in different settings.

> Sh. contributes with confidence in all situations. She often offers explanations and reports back when other children are still fumbling for words. She has the capacity to order her thoughts quickly and she has a very wide English vocabulary. She listens carefully and reasons logically in discussions and helps and supports other children in the group. She is a very competent translator/interpreter and frequently can give explanations in both Sylheti and English to help others. She enjoys talking to adults both known and unknown and is quick to recognize and appreciate a pun.

What experiences and teaching have helped/would help development in this area? Record outcomes of any discussion with head teacher, other staff, or parents.

what is new.

In analysing bilingual children's progress in using English, it will be important to take account of the length of time they have had access to it. For example, some children may encounter English for the first time in the classroom; others may come to school already very experienced with using it — English may be one of the languages spoken at home, or they may have learned it at school in another country.

Central to what constitutes development and progress in talking and listening in the Primary Language Record is the notion of children's growing control and experience of their language or languages. Gradually they develop the power for expressing meanings and ideas in their heads in the ways they want to – both for themselves as individuals, and for exploring and refining with others. In assessing children's growing competence in talking and listening it will therefore be important to respond first of all to what they say, rather than to their styles of speech. It is important to realise that judgements made about children's spoken language are sometimes mere social judgements about the way they talk – particularly the accent they use – rather than anything more fundamental about their ability to express the meanings that are important to them.

For development to take place children need the challenge of new ideas and concepts, as well as social settings that give support for working on them. Any assessment about children's development and progress in talking will need to be matched against the opportunities which are provided in the classroom for that to happen.

Assessing spoken language

The importance of talk in the classroom has been acknowledged as an important dimension in children's learning and development since some of the earliest reports on state education. A continuing recognition of talk in learning is reflected in the recent setting up of the National Oracy Project under the SCDC. But adequate ways of mapping children's spoken language development have always proved elusive, mainly because of the complexity of what it is that is being analysed.

In general in recent years there have been two main approaches to assessing children's spoken language, each influenced by changes in thinking in linguistic theory. The first is a grammatical/structural approach, and involves listing some features of the grammatical system of the language, and checking which ones children can use. This was used for example in the late 60s

and early 70s to assess the language of children enrolled in some of the first Headstart programmes in the USA; it often meant that young children were 'taught' grammatical structures of the language they already knew. This approach to assessment has also been commonly used until quite recently in monitoring the development of bilingual children's spoken English. The difficulty with such a framework is that it can only provide a relatively crude list of some of the grammatical features of a language, and ignores the subtleties of language in use in a real context. In the past, if children have been observed not to be using particular features, it has been assumed that they do not know them, when usually it has been the context which has influenced the choices they have made. Moreover such lists take on meanings not originally intended – they come to be seen as a path of development rather than a mere list for describing features. The use of a limited framework like this was one of the reasons so many children were labelled linguistically deprived during the 1970s. Happily the work of sociolinguists such as William Labov in the USA, with its focus on the power of the social context in children's performance, began to influence ideas about their spoken language, and made clear the inadequacies of structural/grammatical checklists.

A second approach which has been influential for assessing spoken language development and which also stems from the research of sociolinguists has been one which looks at the functions of language – how children *use* language. In *Learning How to Mean*, the British linguist M.A.K. Halliday outlines a functional/interactional model for understanding

children's language acquisition and development. He suggests there are six major functions through which children learn to express their ideas and meanings, and in so doing acquire and develop their language. This has been an important theoretical model. Where it has been copied in a simplistic way for tracing language development in the classroom, this too has become restrictive. As with the grammatical-structural framework, assessment through functions has tended to emphasise what children *cannot* do with language rather than what they *can* do, and has largely ignored the effect of social context on use.

An approach that *has* recognised the influence of the social context in observing children's talk has developed from the work of Douglas Barnes and his colleagues, who collected and analysed examples of secondary-age children working together. Children's uses of language in small-group conversations were described for their social and cognitive functions: conversation moves (e.g. initiating, responding), logical process (e.g. categorising, evaluating), social skills, (e.g. encouraging another's contribution), cognitive strategies (e.g. setting up hypotheses), and metalinguistics (e.g. monitoring their own use of language). Some of these categories have informed the suggestions for analysing children's spoken language in the record.

Social settings in the classrooms

The classroom offers many opportunities for children working and talking together in a range of social settings. These may be small groups (pairs, threes and fours) structured so that children can work together in a range of curriculum contexts, for example, discussing a poem, drafting a story, making a book, problem-solving in maths and science investigations. They also include more informal groupings where children come together spontaneously to work, for example, role-playing in the Home Corner, or a similar setting. 'Large formal occasions' will include such events as the presentation of a class's work for an Assembly to the whole school, groups and individuals sharing aspects of project work with the rest of the class, and whole class discussions.

The demands of the small group, where the context has been explored together, is different from the demands of the more formal occasion. Children need opportunities for experiencing the demands of both situations, and will need to be observed working in both. A small group provides an easier context for a child to explore ideas and possibilities, for being tentative about what s/he means and understands. Hesitations, pauses, and rephrasing are all part of this process and are evidence of the ways in which a speaker is simultaneously monitoring what s/he is saying, and thinking ahead to what s/he wants to say next.

The whole class situation can be daunting for some children. Experience gained in small groups, however, will give children confidence to talk in more formal settings. Children's confidence in themselves as talkers will vary and they may need sympathetic support in both kinds of contexts if they are to contribute confidently. It is important to recognise also that individuals have their own personal ways of participating in conversations. Sometimes children who appear shy or silent may actually be listening hard, and will contribute when they are ready to do so.

Ideally all children should be able to hold their own in classroom and group discussions, feel secure enough to make a contribution in different working contexts, and be able to frame their language for the audience they are talking to. It is also important to remember that children's talk in small groups will be affected by the membership of the group – by personalities that are compatible or not, by relationships between girls and boys, by attitudes to race and culture. Children's skills as communicators are partly to do with their ability to use their language for expressing their understanding of activities they are involved in, and partly to do with listening and responding to contributions others are making. Being a good communicator is not necessarily to do with the amount of talking a child does – a well-timed and thoughtful contribution to a discussion from someone who has been listening hard can be as valuable in taking forward the thinking of a group as more lengthy contributions.

In some classrooms, too, children sharing a first language other than English may want to explore ideas together in that language in their small group work. It is important for children to feel that discussion in that language is valued, and has a part to play in their learning and the work of the classroom.

Drama and social settings

A powerful way of extending the range of social contexts in the real life of the classroom is through drama:

– by creating an imagined reality different roles can be adopted and different demands made on the children's language. They can, for example, be servants in the palace awaiting an angry King Minos, or they can be the King. Depending on who they are they will be able to choose the appropriate language register and ideas for that role.

– many monolingual English-speaking children come to school speaking a variety of English different from their teachers. There can be both class and regional differences. It is important in school that children are encouraged to use the language they bring from home, and to stay confident in its use. Awareness of differences between varieties can be developed through discussion, drama and dramatic play, and children encouraged to build on those they know and to explore those that are new to them.

– by working alongside children in creating imagined realities a teacher can change her status in the classroom, enabling children to talk with each other and with her in a way which is often difficult in the real life of the classroom, where the power relationships between adults and children are usually fixed.

Curriculum contexts for children's development in talking and listening

Some of the most influential discussions about the importance of talk in the classroom were by teachers of English and primary teachers working together in the National Association for the Teaching of English (NATE). These were recorded in *Language, the Learner and the School* in 1969. There were two important strands running through this and subsequent publications (including the Bullock Report in 1975). One was the social dimension of classroom interaction and the teacher's role in it. The second was children learning to use their language as a tool for learning through all areas of the curriculum. Talk (as well, of course, as reading and writing) does not take place in a vacuum. People talk about *something*.

For children in school the content of talk will include the new ideas and challenges that the curriculum offers. It is through talking about those ideas with others in their own words and in their own way that children can begin to understand new ideas and make them their own. And it is the wide range of opportunities for exploring different contexts and purposes for talk offered by the curriculum, that makes it a powerful base for children to develop their skills as talkers and listeners. For talk changes with the learning contexts in which it takes place: the language used in telling a story is likely to be different from language used for discussion in a science investigation; planning a mathematics investigation will be different from conversation around the sand tray, and so on.

Drama in curriculum contexts

Within the curriculum drama has always been known to have special significance for children's spoken language development. Through drama it is possible to create opportunities for children to use what they already know about the world (their understanding and experience of it) in an imagined context, and through it to explore issues and concepts important for them and the communities they live in. They can find ways of expressing themselves that draw on and extend their everyday use of language because they are actively involved in a situation which has meaning and purpose for them. Drama here is not only about theatre or performance skills, for to restrict children to the acting-out of a known story or to the learning of lines for a play is to limit the opportunities for talk that drama offers. Children need to be involved in the planning and shaping of the drama and not simply engaged in acting-out a pre-set narrative.

B2 Reading

Like the sections on 'Talking and listening' and 'Writing', the section on 'Reading' is to be completed in the Spring Term. It is intended to give teachers opportunity to record observations and analyses of a child's progress and development as a reader. Information can be gathered from previous records, the teacher's own records, knowledge of the child's reading experiences outside school, the child's view of her/himself as a reader and the teacher's detailed observations noted in the observation and sample sheet.

Additional pieces of information can be recorded in Part C during the Summer Term.

Reading and language development

Reading cannot be examined in total isolation from talking, listening and writing, so it is important to consider each child in the context of her/his language and learning experiences. Furthermore many children will be learning to talk, read and/or write in a second or even third language and it is crucial that their learning in more than one language is supported, developed and understood as valuable and enriching.

The view of reading adopted in the record is one which acknowledges the fact that learning to read has much in common with learning to talk.

B2 Reading

Please comment on the child's progress and development as a reader in English and/or other community languages: the stage at which the child is operating (refer to the reading scales on pages 26-27); the range, quantity and variety of reading in all areas of the curriculum; the child's pleasure and involvement in story and reading, alone or with others; the range of strategies used when reading and the child's ability to reflect critically on what is read.

At the beginning of the year C. was reluctant to move away from a small number of books which she read accurately. Since she has gained confidence as a reader C. is tackling more demanding print. She is a Beginner reader / Non-fluent reader on the reading scale 1. C. is developing quite a number of known words in her reading. She is also developing strategies – picture/meaning/context cues and she can also use some initial sounds and her one-to-one correspondence is good. The range of books she is happy to read has increased dramatically since she has become more sure of herself. C. enjoys listening to stories and being read to.

What experiences and teaching have helped/would help development in this area? Record outcomes of any discussion with head teacher, other staff, or parents.

Encourage her to continue choosing a wide range of books that will stretch her.
Encourage her knowledge of initial sounds.

B2 Reading

Please comment on the child's progress and development as a reader in English and/or other community languages: the stage at which the child is operating (refer to the reading scales on pages 26-27); the range, quantity and variety of reading in all areas of the curriculum; the child's pleasure and involvement in story and reading, alone or with others; the range of strategies used when reading and the child's ability to reflect critically on what is read.

A. is becoming far more confident in tackling known and some unknown texts. He is progressing towards being a 'Moderately fluent' reader and is making steady progress. He is developing strategies such as checking guesses, initial sounds, picture cues, and is beginning to read in phrases. Although still below the class average, A. is highly motivated and shows a sound interest and pleasure in reading. He attempts a wide variety of books in terms of subject matter and complexity.

What experiences and teaching have helped/would help development in this area? Record outcomes of any discussion with head teacher, other staff, or parents.

— Access to reading material that is within his capability to tackle alone to really boost his confidence and increase his motivation.
— He needs lots of opportunity to share reading with an adult and more interesting and challenging reading material.
— A. needs opportunities to discuss/explore books.

▲ **C** *Reception class — girl*
Languages: **English**

This example shows clearly how the wording of this section and the accompanying notes in the handbook have helped the teacher to structure her comments. She has found a way of talking about C's growing competence as a reader in clear and cogent terms which will be of value to other members of staff and to C's parents.

◀ **A** *Middle Infants — boy*
Languages: **English**

There is a strong feeling that although A. is still at the early stages of reading his involvement and enthusiasm for a wide range of books are likely to be key factors in his further development. The teacher has made some very helpful recommendations about ways of supporting the child's progress: developing his autonomy as a reader on the one hand, while at the same time, increasing the opportunities he has for reading and discussing with other children and adults.

A child's capacity for learning language will be one of the greatest assets in learning to read. Bilingual children will have demonstrated already their language learning powers, and how they use what they know about one language to learn another. They process and reprocess the language they hear, speculate, check, confirm or reject – continually refining their understanding of the less familiar language in the light of new information.

Over the last twenty years or so there have been several fundamental developments in our understanding of what is involved in learning to read. It may be helpful to review some of the changes that have taken place in thinking about the subject in order to see how the psycholinguistic approach to reading, implicit in the record, has evolved.

Teaching and learning to read: a historical perspective

In the early part of this century many psychologists concentrated almost exclusively on studying reading as a perceptual process (decoding print). It was not until the middle of the century that linguists began to suggest that there were other elements to consider in the learning-to-read process. So in reading research there was a movement away from a narrow concentration on the visual characteristics of individual words towards using children's knowledge and experience of oral language as a powerful basis for literacy learning. The language-experience approach, as it eventually became known, stressed the importance of using children's first-hand experiences and natural interests as motivating forces in helping them to acquire and develop reading and writing skills. Children's descriptions of particular experiences were written down and became reading resources. As children became more confident they were expected to copy their own dictated sentences. In 1970 *Breakthrough to Literacy* was published in this country as part of a Schools Council project; it drew on language-experience approaches and translated them into a systematic programme.

Psycholinguistics and reading

In North America in the 60's and 70's psycholinguistic research focused on bringing together all that was now known about how children acquired language in order to consider how they learned to read. Kenneth Goodman and colleagues came to refer to the learning-to-read process as a psycholinguistic guessing game: research findings demonstrated so clearly the way in which even beginning readers brought all their linguistic knowledge and experience of life to the task of processing text. Thus the 'errors' children make as they read aloud became more favourably known as miscues; miscue analysis, the study of oral reading behaviour, emerged as a nucleus for a whole new way of thinking about what was involved in learning to read.

Frank Smith argued that as children learn to talk by talking so they learn to read by reading. The teacher's task was to make reading easier. He further proposed that learning to read was not

made easy by breaking down the process into a series of component parts nor by presenting children with contrived or over-simplified texts. To develop increasing control over any new learning process the learner had to take on the whole activity and make sense of it. In *Reading*, he suggested that there were two basic needs for apprentice readers:

> 'the availability of interesting material that makes sense to the learner and an understanding and more experienced reader as a guide.'

Psycholinguists articulated the ways in which the reader draws upon the cue systems already available in written language in order to make sense of texts by using all the available cues. These are:

semantic cues (meaning cues)
— using knowledge and experience of stories and of written texts to predict events, phrases and words and above all to make the text make sense

syntactic cues (language cues)
— drawing on knowledge and experience of patterns in oral and written language to predict text

grapho-phonic cues (print cues)
— using knowledge and experience of relationships between sounds and symbols to read particular words

Obviously the reader applies a combination of strategies in order to read and the process is a cycle of predicting, sampling, confirming, and correcting as Constance Weaver shows in this diagram from *Psycholinguistics and Reading*:

READING STRATEGIES

		Predict	Sample	Confirm/Correct
LANGUAGE CUES	Syntactic			
	Semantic			
	Grapho-phonic			

This research and in particular the work and thinking of the advocates of language-experience approaches, and of psycholinguists like Kenneth Goodman, was brought to the attention of a wide audience in the Bullock Report published in 1975. The Report was also important in setting reading in the context of language and learning so that it was no longer envisaged as an isolated skill.

Home and school

In the 80's one of the most important developments in the field of reading has been the

growing emphasis placed on home-school links, on children's knowledge of literacy before schooling, and on contributions that all parents make to their children's development as readers.

We are now more aware of the broad knowledge of literacy that children acquire before coming to school. Contrary to what used to be thought, it is now known that the language of all children, except those with severe language learning difficulties, is an adequate basis for literacy learning.

The research programme which produced convincing evidence for this was the Bristol Language Development Research Project, which studied a group of children from infancy and into primary school. Gordon Wells, the director of the project, also sought to discover whether there were any particular pre-school activities/experiences that contributed to children's educational achievement at primary school level. The results were clear-cut: *listening to stories* was significantly associated with children's development as readers and writers:

> 'Stories read aloud and discussed in a way which encourages reflection upon their own experience and imaginative exploration of the world created through the language of the text are probably the best way of helping young children to begin to develop these abilities.'

> *Gordon Wells*
> *Language, Learning and Education*

Learning to read

As a result of these research findings, we are now in a better position to consider how children learn to read and the kinds of classroom environments that support this learning.

A child learns to talk in the company of others; it is an interactive process where meanings are explored, shared and developed. So it is with reading. In the early stages when an adult (or older child) reads to the child it is normal for the child to ask questions or make comments about the pictures, the print and the nature of the text itself. Through this kind of talk, the conversations that naturally surround shared reading and the sharing of books, children come to know more about what is involved in being a reader.

To be literate means many things and children are growing up in a world where there are ever-increasing demands made upon them in the field of literacy. Children have to learn what to read and what not to read depending on individual needs and interests. In this technological age, at home and in the world outside home and school, print abounds; it serves many purposes, often of a purely functional nature, e.g. signs in the supermarket, the bus timetable, television advertisements. So children come to school with some knowledge and understanding of print and very often in more than one language. But as Margaret Meek said in *Learning to Read*:

> '… literacy doesn't begin and end in the official sphere of social contracts… Good readers are more than successful print-scanners and retrievers of factual information. They find in books the depth and breadth of human experience.'

So it is essential that we invite children to be members of literate communities in the fullest sense.

The role of texts in learning to read

It seems clear that texts have a key role to play in a child's development as a reader. Books that make up a child's repertoire of known texts should be books that are worth returning to again and again. Stories and rhymes that stem from oral and literate traditions are arguably the most powerful source of texts for apprentice readers.

Children will have their own favourites but it is remarkable how often certain texts (e.g. *Rosie's Walk, Where the Wild Things Are, Bringing the Rain to Kapiti Plain, Mr. Gumpy's Outing, The Very Hungry Caterpillar, Bears in the Night*) are mentioned as being particularly popular with young readers. Books like this share:

   – a strong story
   – a lively, rhythmical text
   – powerful, imaginative content
   – memorable language
   – interesting illustrations, that complement the text
   – humour
   – language that is not contrived or unnatural (as it sometimes is in published reading schemes)

Bilingual children can expect to find in schools an increasing number of memorable stories, such as those mentioned above, published in dual language editions, and stories published in a number of community/home languages. The importance of including a wide selection of quality books from a variety of cultural settings and in a variety of languages cannot be over-emphasised. This wide selection of books will offer valuable support to bilingual children in learning to read in more than one

language and in widening all children's experiences of other people's linguistic and literary heritages.

As well as commercially published texts, children's own texts play a powerful role in developing reading ability. These texts may be dictated and scribed by another child or member of staff or may be written by children themselves. The written texts (in English and/or other community languages) can be accompanied by illustrations or designs and made into books. Subsequently these books become part of the classroom's reading resources offering a wide range of reading experiences for all children.

Reading aloud to children and learning to read

It seems that reading aloud to children is of the utmost importance in supporting their development as readers.

A child who is learning to read and who is read to frequently builds up a repertoire of known texts which s/he wants to return to again and again. On each occasion and over time the child plays a more active role in the reading. S/he is familiar with the story-line, with the tune on the page and has a natural inclination to predict; so s/he becomes the story-teller and re-enacts the text. It is the familiarisation that helps a child develop a growing awareness of what is involved in being able to do it for her/himself.

Similarly a more experienced reader will gain much pleasure and learn a great deal from being read to. S/he will develop an understanding of different genres and different styles, will come to know and enjoy an increasing number of writers and will experience certain books that otherwise s/he might never encounter.

Growing in confidence

With continued support – being read to, by teachers and other experienced readers in an out of school, discussing texts, being invited to read familiar phrases – a child develops an understanding that it is the print that carries the message: s/he becomes more aware of the significant features of print itself. Over time and with experience – the experience of reading familiar texts – the child's confidence and competence grow. S/he plays an increasingly autonomous role, understanding the interaction of picture and text; taking risks with print by making informed guesses based on semantic, syntactic and grapho-phonic information and using a number of strategies that s/he is developing to try out hypotheses and to confirm or reject them as new knowledge is added to the old.

Over a period the child's reading strategies

and the language cues of print begin to mesh and the child takes on more and more of the reading for her/himself, bringing to the activity all s/he knows and can do to make the text meaningful.

Moving into silent reading

Some time in the primary school, often in the infant department, most children move from reading aloud to reading silently. The transition period is an important one where, in the initial stages, a child sub-vocalises the words reading at the same pace as if s/he were reading aloud. With experience and maturity, the words become 'thoughts in the head' and the rate of reading increases. During this time a child still needs support and guidance. S/he also needs time to browse and to engage in silent reading for sustained periods of time.

The difficulty with silent reading from a teacher's standpoint is that it is naturally a private process so teachers have to find ways of working with children that support their development. Group discussion is often a good way of extending the understanding and experiences of books that have been read silently, as are opportunities to explore stories, for instance, through drama. In order that children can feel confident about themselves as readers, their tentative as well as their carefully considered responses to texts should be valued and encouraged. As they experience a greater variety of books and reading material across all areas of the curriculum they will need support in coming to realise that different texts demand different styles of reading.

An experienced reader

As the child becomes more fluent and experienced across the wide range of reading demands that exist in the primary classroom s/he will be willing to take on more extended and more challenging texts. Illustrations become less crucial in supporting understanding, although this is not to underestimate the power and vitality of picture books for older children. With encouragement, the child will become more critical of what s/he reads, and what writers have to say. S/he will become more able to question and/or admire aspects of content, form and function. S/he will come to realise that there exist in some texts elements of prejudice and will be able to recognise and criticise texts or illustrations that are biased. Developing readers will also be extending their understanding of texts by detecting elements like ambiguity or irony.

B2

Development in reading and the reading scales

There are, therefore, generalisations that can be made about what constitutes growth and development in reading. It is important to think of development in reading as development along a continuum; in their growth as readers children initially move from *dependence to independence*.

To begin with, learners depend on an adult or more experienced reader to read the text aloud to them. But as their knowledge of texts and of written language(s) grows, they gradually become more confident about tackling, in the first instance, familiar texts, and then unfamiliar ones for themselves.

Becoming a reader: reading scale 1

The diagram that follows shows in more detail aspects of a child's move along the *dependence-independence* continuum. The scale was devised in the first instance to help teachers of children in the top infant age range log individual development using this reading scale with a set of operational definitions to support their decisions. The scale can however be used as a base for thinking about children's progress across a wider age range; it offers some helpful

ways of describing what a child is able to do, with increasing ease, on the road to becoming a fluent reader. This scale can also be used to identify children whose reading development is causing some concern. If a child at the top of the infant school is described as a beginner reader or a non-fluent reader on this scale, s/he may require particular support and help.

Using the reading scale – top infants and first-year juniors

As part of an assessment procedure it is proposed that in the Spring Term of the top infant and first-year junior age groups each child's development is recorded using this reading scale and noted in section B2 of the Primary Language Record, for example:

Moderately fluent reader (date)

Subsequent information on a child's development as a reader can be recorded in Part C in the Summer Term.

Teachers will appreciate that this scale is particularly useful for top infants and first-year juniors but it may also be helpful in considering the reading of children in the general age range of six to eight. There may also be individual cases where it is appropriate for an older child who is not yet reading independently.

Bilingual development and the reading scale

Many bilingual children will be becoming readers in more than one language. Bilingual development/community language teachers will be able to provide a great deal of feedback about literacy in first languages and discuss with the class teachers strategies that each child is developing on the way to becoming biliterate. In schools where there is no support for particular bilingual children, class teachers can observe and listen to children reading aloud in other languages and discover a great deal about them as readers (see Appendix C: Informal Assessment). This kind of information can be recorded in B2.

Some bilingual children will be more competent as readers in their first language, others not. Whichever is the case it is valuable, where possible, for teachers who share the child's language or who have the help of bilingual development/community language teachers to log children's development in both languages. The reading scales can obviously be useful here. So, for instance, a child whose first language is Turkish may be a *fluent reader* in Turkish, but because of little experience of reading in English might be described as a *non-fluent reader* in English. It will be important in assessing a child's reading in English, to note also how long s/he has been learning English.

Adapting the scale

There will be times when a teacher feels that for one reason or another the definitions do not adequately describe what a child can do as a reader. It is reasonable to expect that there will be other signs that are indicative of development and it is important that these signs are noted in B2. Furthermore there will be instances when a child seems to be moving between one set of definitions and another; it is also relevant to record this information, for example:

Beginner reader/Non-fluent reader

After the age of eight the scale will probably become less useful as a reliable guide for logging and describing reading development. For older and experienced readers, therefore, a second scale has been developed, which focuses, in greater detail, on the qualitative aspects of children's developing experiences in reading across the curriculum areas.

Becoming a reader: reading scale 1

DEPENDENCE ↑

Beginner reader 1	Does not have enough successful strategies for tackling print independently. Relies on having another person read the text aloud. May still be unaware that text carries meaning.
Non-fluent reader 2	Tackling known and predictable texts with growing confidence but still needing support with new and unfamiliar ones. Growing ability to predict meanings and developing strategies to check predictions against other cues such as the illustrations and the print itself.
Moderately fluent reader 3	Well-launched on reading but still needing to return to a familiar range of texts. At the same time beginning to explore new kinds of texts independently. Beginning to read silently.
Fluent reader 4	A capable reader who now approaches familiar texts with confidence but still needs support with unfamiliar materials. Beginning to draw inferences from books and stories read independently. Chooses to read silently.
Exceptionally fluent reader 5	An avid and independent reader, who is making choices from a wide range of material. Able to appreciate nuances and subtleties in text.

↓ INDEPENDENCE

Experience as a reader across the curriculum: reading scale 2

The first reading scale is concerned with a reader's journey from dependence to independence; it is a *fluency scale*. The second reading scale focuses on a child's increasing involvement with a diverse range and variety of reading materials; it is *a scale of experience*.

The diagram that follows illustrates in some detail elements of a child's developing experience as a reader. In the junior school years children engage with a much greater selection of books and texts – fiction and non-fiction books, and computers. . . . It is crucial that they are supported in their endeavours to take on the multi-faceted reading demands of a junior school curriculum. So in assessing second, third and fourth year children's progress and development as readers, we need to consider that in addition to a growing ability to be able to read silently, fluently and with ease, there is a widening of reading horizons where the notion of range and variety play an increasingly important part in children's interactions with texts.

As their ability and experience increase, children become more skilful at knowing what to read and what not to read; in other words they are more discerning and experienced as readers and realise that different texts require different reading approaches. The *scale of experience* is therefore intended to help teachers note the quality of a child's experiences as a reader, and not merely the amount they have read.

Using the scale of experience – second, third and fourth year juniors

As part of an assessment procedure it is proposed that in the Spring Term of the second, third and fourth year junior age groups each child's development is recorded using this reading scale and noted in Part B2 of the Primary Language Record, for example:

Moderately experienced reader (date)

Subsequent information on a child's development as a reader can be recorded in Part C in the Summer Term.

Teachers will probably find that this scale is particularly useful for children of nine, ten and eleven years of age although there may be cases where this is not so; occasionally it will be helpful when considering a seven or eight year-old's progress.

Many bilingual children will be developing as readers in more than one language. Some will be more competent in English than in their community language, others not. Whichever is the case, and as was suggested for the younger age range, it is helpful to chart children's development in both languages where possible.

For more detail on charting reading development in more than one language see the previous section.

If there are occasions when the teacher feels that for one reason or another the definitions do not adequately describe what a child is able to do as a reader then it will be valuable if s/he records any relevant observations in B2. In addition s/he may think that a child fits between one set of descriptions and another, in which case s/he may like to record the information like this:

Experienced reader/Exceptionally experienced reader (date)

Experience as a reader across the curriculum: reading scale 2

INEXPERIENCED ▲

Inexperienced reader 1	Experience as a reader has been limited. Generally chooses to read very easy and familiar texts where illustrations play an important part. Has difficulty with any unfamiliar material and yet may be able to read own dictated texts confidently. Needs a great deal of support with the reading demands of the classroom. Over-dependent on one strategy when reading aloud; often reads word by word. Rarely chooses to read for pleasure.
Less experienced reader 2	Developing fluency as a reader and reading certain kinds of material with confidence. Usually chooses short books with simple narrative shapes and with illustrations and may read these silently; often re-reads favourite books. Reading for pleasure often includes comics and magazines. Needs help with the reading demands of the classroom and especially with using reference and information books.
Moderately experienced reader 3	A confident reader who feels at home with books. Generally reads silently and is developing stamina as a reader. Is able to read for longer periods and cope with more demanding texts, including children's novels. Willing to reflect on reading and often uses reading in own learning. Selects books independently and can use information books and materials for straightforward reference purposes, but still needs help with unfamiliar material, particularly non-narrative prose.
Experienced reader 4	A self-motivated, confident and experienced reader who may be pursuing particular interests through reading. Capable of tackling some demanding texts and can cope well with the reading of the curriculum. Reads thoughtfully and appreciates shades of meaning. Capable of locating and drawing on a variety of sources in order to research a topic independently.
Exceptionally experienced reader 5	An enthusiastic and reflective reader who has strong established tastes in fiction and/or non-fiction. Enjoys pursuing own reading interests independently. Can handle a wide range and variety of texts, including some adult material. Recognises that different kinds of texts require different styles of reading. Able to evaluate evidence drawn from a variety of information sources. Is developing critical awareness as a reader.

▼ EXPERIENCED

Some explanations of terms used in the 'Reading' section

'. . . stage at which the child is operating . . .'

It is hoped that the two reading scales will help teachers to identify the stage at which a child is operating as s/he becomes a more independent and experienced reader. The descriptions will enable teachers to identify a reader's strengths, and to pinpoint the areas where support is needed. More detailed analysis can be obtained from sampling the child's reading using a running record, making a miscue analysis or through informal assessment (see observation and sample sheet).

'. . . the range, quantity and variety of reading in all areas of the curriculum . . .'

In school and at home children read for a variety of purposes. Many aspects of the curriculum will involve reading. Over a period of time a child may be reading different kinds of fiction, poems, comics/magazines, newspapers, and jokes, as well as instructions for making something, explanations of a mathematical problem or concept, reports on scientific topics, computer programs and information/text-books.

Children may not read equally across the range but at different times will need to read more in one area that another, as well as developing preferences and special interests within the range.

'. . . pleasure and involvement in story and reading, alone or with others . . .'

If children are to develop as readers there must be personal involvement in reading. The pleasures of reading often begin as shared pleasures and arise from reading with an adult. When a child experiences the emotional satisfaction of involvement in story, s/he is likely to want to read

more. Even when children are reading quite independently, the satisfactions they find in books can be increased by being shared with other readers. When there is time and space for this kind of sharing in the classroom, and as children encounter a widening variety of books, the range of their personal reading choices will grow.

'. . . range of strategies used when reading . . .'

Observation of a child reading silently will reveal some of the ways in which s/he approaches the task, and it is possible to identify some strategies being used. When the child reads aloud other strategies may be revealed. The teacher needs to notice:

- whether the child uses illustration (initially to help retell the story, later to check guesses)
- whether the child makes use of the context to help work out the meaning; does what s/he read make sense?
- whether the child reads in meaningful 'chunks', or word by word?
- whether the child uses the structure of language to help work out the meaning
- whether the child uses knowledge about books and written language to help work out meaning
- whether the child uses knowledge of what words/letters look or sound like to help work out unknown words
- whether s/he makes a good guess at unknown words or waits to be told
- whether s/he is using several strategies to get meaning from the text or has a heavy dependence on one strategy (e.g. phonic analysis)
- whether the child self-corrects, and seems to be monitoring her/his own reading

The reading samples will help to identify the strategies a child uses when reading.

'. . . ability to reflect critically on what is read . . .'

Children need to talk about books in order to clarify their ideas, to relate reading to experience and to reflect on what they have read. This is the real meaning of comprehension. They need to understand that different readers may respond differently to the same book, and that books may be biased, inaccurate or inadequate.

The greater the child's experience of reading a wide variety of texts, the better s/he will be able to evaluate what is read and to make informed choices.

◀ **Ay** *2nd year junior — girl*
Languages: **Sylheti, Bengali, English**

There is a great deal of information here about Ay's growing competence as a reader, reading in English and Bengali. The teacher recognises the importance of supporting the child's literacy development in both languages, knowing that development in one will support development in the other. There are significant references to the wide range of strategies Ay. uses when reading aloud, her growing ability to read between the lines and her increasing preference for silent reading.

B2 Reading

Please comment on the child's progress and development as a reader in English and/or other community languages: the stage at which the child is operating (refer to the reading scales on pp....); the range, quantity and variety of reading in all areas of the curriculum; the child's pleasure and involvement in story and reading, alone or with others; the range of strategies used when reading and the child's ability to reflect critically on what is read.

Ay. is a fluent reader in English and Bengali and one of the more able readers in the 2nd year. She seeks meaning from the texts she reads and grasps understanding from sentences read or by reading on. She uses grapho-phonic cues with unknown words, self-corrects and is able to retain newly introduced vocabulary. She stumbles on longer words, nominally longer verbs (eg. polishing, managing) and as she continues to read so enthusiastically she will

B2 (cont) combat this difficulty. Ay. is much more critical about books this term and selects with more interest. She is more confident now in reading aloud and enjoys reading to her friends and in assembly. Ay. is also reading silently more often. When she reads in Bengali she translates readily.

What experiences and teaching have helped/would help development in this area? Record outcomes of any discussion with head teacher, other staff, or parents.

Continue to offer a range of interesting books with humorous storylines and with understandable developments in text. Also develop reference book skills (index, glossary, information retrieval.)

B3 Writing

Like the sections on 'Talking and listening', and 'Reading', the section on 'Writing' is to be filled in during the Spring Term. This section in the record is intended to give teachers space to summarise their observations about a child's writing up to this time.

Teachers completing this section of the record will want to draw on their own informal records of a child's writing development and may also have completed writing samples on the observations and sample sheet.

There follows a general introduction to the section, and detailed notes on some of the headings.

Writing: changing theory and practice

Writing is a language mode which is currently attracting a great deal of interest and attention. Much more is now known about how children learn to write, and about the writing process itself. This increased awareness has been reflected in changes in classroom practice, *away from* copying, 'exercises', and short one-off pieces of writing and *towards* writing workshop approaches which encourage children's independence as writers, give them ample time to work on their writing, and often lead to the 'publication' of children's work. In multilingual classrooms there is also greater appreciation of the fact that children may be literate in more than one language, and there are more opportunities to write in community languages.

In this climate of changing theory and practice, what generalisations can be made about how children learn to write and about their progress and development in writing?

What children know before they come to school

In writing, as with other language modes, we are now more conscious of how much children already know before they ever come to school. In their earliest writing they draw on their existing language resources and their knowledge. This knowledge is of several different kinds:

a) knowledge of spoken language
b) knowledge of story
c) knowledge of written language
d) knowledge of print

a) Knowledge of spoken language

'The child must learn that one can draw not only objects but also speech'

Lev Vygotsky

Spoken language is the first and most important resource that young writers have. It is the foundation for all of a child's later understanding of written language systems. This is one reason for the importance of supporting the first languages of young bilingual children.

The spoken language of all children is adequate as a foundation for their written language development; initially it will be normal and desirable for children to write as they speak and for speech and dialect forms to appear in their writings. As they read more and their linguistic range grows, they will, in addition, begin to make an increasingly confident use of written standard forms.

b) Knowledge of story

Many children have a very well-developed knowledge of the shapes and structures of stories, either from being read to or from belonging to a culture where oral story-telling is general. These understandings can feed directly into their own story-writing.

c) Knowledge of written language

'Written language has to be more explicit than speech because it stands alone'

K. Perera

Written language is both more *explicit* and more *complex in its structures* than spoken language. Children may have considerable experience of written language even before they come to write it because of their experiences of being read to. 'Talking like a book' is a sign that children are beginning to enjoy the tunes of written language.

d) Knowledge of print

Even very young children may have an extensive knowledge of print, simply from being alive in a world which contains so much of it. In any urban environment they are surrounded by signs, notices, packaging and adverts; when they watch television, print is always appearing on the screen. Bilingual children may be becoming familiar with the appearance of more than one script. Many children begin to form their first hypotheses about sound-symbol relationships from these experiences, and in their earliest writing they often try out their knowledge of print.

◀ | C | *Reception infants — girl*
Languages: **English**

In completing the record for this reception infant child the teacher notes many encouraging signs of progress. C's understanding of the writing system is developing rapidly and she is beginning to write independently and with enjoyment.

B3 Writing
Please comment on the child's progress and development as a writer in English and/or other community languages: the degree of confidence and independence as a writer; the range, quantity and variety of writing in all areas of the curriculum; the child's pleasure and involvement in writing both narrative and non-narrative, alone and in collaboration with others; the influence of reading on the child's writing; growing understanding of written language, its conventions and spelling.

C. enjoys writing and is building up a small number of known words. She is beginning to gain confidence, to be an independent writer and to attempt phonic approximations of words. She has an understanding of written language conventions — awareness of differences between words and letters and between upper and lower case. Her handwriting is mature and well-formed.

What experiences and teaching have helped/would help development in this area? Record outcomes of any discussion with head teacher, other staff, or parents.

Encourage her to continue to write independently and to have a 'go' at unknown words.

Make resources available. e.g. word banks, lists, other books etc.

29

Learning to write

Learning to write, like learning to read, is a journey, a journey from dependence to independence. Initially a child needs the help and support of another person, usually an adult, in order to write, support which can be gradually withdrawn as the child takes over more and more of the process.

Composition and transcription

But writing is not one unified process. The act of writing can be divided into two distinct parts:

1) composition (the actual creation of a text); and
2) transcription (the writing down of the text).

Frank Smith, who formulated this distinction, broke the writing process down into the different jobs which come under these two headings:

COMPOSITION (author)	TRANSCRIPTION (secretary)
Getting ideas	Physical effort of writing
Selecting words	Spelling
Grammar	Capitalization Punctuation Paragraphs Legibility

Young children can obviously compose long before they can transcribe. Most of the problems connected with learning to 'write' are problems to do with transcription and most approaches to teaching writing have been ways of dealing with transcription.

There are two main ways in which teachers now help children who are learning to write:

a) by making transcription easier
b) by encouraging independence

a) Making transcription easier

Many 'methods' of teaching writing, from copying under the teacher's writing to *Breakthrough to Literacy*, have been ways of helping children to cope with transcription. Unfortunately such methods do not always take account of children's

▶ | A | *Middle infants — girl*
*Languages: **English***

A. is developing rapidly as a writer, and her interest in writing narrative, both personal and fictional, is made very clear here. Retelling — either the story of the day's events, or the story of a book she has enjoyed — obviously offers her a good way of structuring extended texts. The teacher notes the ways in which her skills in transcription are also developing well.

existing knowledge and may also restrict the range of what they can compose. However there are still many ways in which teachers share some of the burden of transcription with children, and thus enable them to compose more freely. These include:

Teacher as 'scribe' When children dictate their stories to teachers (or other adults) they can compose at much more length than they would otherwise be able to do, and bring into play their growing knowledge of written language and story forms. This means they appreciate more of the satisfactions and purposes of writing. Teachers may not be able to scribe for the bilingual children in their classes when they write in their first languages, but if other teachers, including bilingual development/community language teachers, and parents are involved then it will be possible to offer them this kind of support.

Shared writing allows several children to collaborate in the making of a text which the teacher scribes. Children can learn a great deal from working on a story with others, and gain knowledge of transcription from watching the teacher do it.

Collaborative writing When children write in pairs or small groups they can help each other compose and can share their transcriptional knowledge.

Word-processing Composing on a word-processor minimises some of the difficulties of transcription – such as handwriting – and allows texts to be corrected easily, so that an attractive final draft can be produced. The word-processor also offers a very good context for collaborative writing. Pairs and small groups of children can easily compose texts together and can pool their knowledge of transcription at the same time.

b) Encouraging independence

In addition to using these ways of making transcription easier, many teachers are now encouraging children to write independently from an early stage. Even in the nursery school children who are given the opportunity to use what they know are able to demonstrate considerable knowledge of the forms of writing, sometimes in more than one script. Given encouragement, they can draw on all this knowledge as they begin to attempt the business of transcription for themselves.

When they are writing independently children may initially simply 'draw writing' or practise known scripts. But as they begin to hypothesise about the way written language works, and learn more about it from their reading, their independent writing begins to approximate more and more closely to standard writing systems. In English it will be normal for children to 'write' texts which look like strings of letters, or in which words are represented by their initial letters, or (later) where words are written as clusters of consonants with the vowels omitted. Early invented spellings are often logical and self-consistent, and it is valuable if children can learn to have a go at spelling words themselves instead of continually asking teachers for words.

B3 Writing
Please comment on the child's progress and development as a writer in English and/or other community languages: the degree of confidence and independence as a writer; the range, quantity and variety of writing in all areas of the curriculum; the child's pleasure and involvement in writing both narrative and non-narrative, alone and in collaboration with others; the influence of reading on the child's writing; growing understanding of written language, its conventions and spelling.

A. prefers to choose her own subjects for writing usually about her family and the day's events. She has chosen twice to re-write favourite stories. The last extended story was a re-write of "Tiddalick" beginning "Once upon a time." A good deal of evidence of sophisticated book language, e.g. 'The animals caused a meeting' and 'the wombat spoke up.' A. uses initial letters, has a fair range of known words, spacing good, varied length of words.

What experiences and teaching have helped/would help development in this area? Record outcomes of any discussion with head teacher, other staff, or parents.

Encourage more factual writing.

Early spellings will develop over time given the right experiences, information and support. Because the English spelling system does present children with particular problems, a special section on spelling in English has been included in this handbook, on pages 33 and 34.

The role of the teacher

Even when children are writing independently they still require support; judgement is needed to decide how to provide this most effectively. Where children are writing in community languages, teachers may have to call on the assistance of other staff, parents or other adults. Without suggesting that a child's own efforts are 'wrong', teachers may need to intervene with help or information, especially if children seem to be getting stuck at a particular stage. The most important form of support, however, will always be the teacher's response to the *content* of the writing, and the sharing of children's writing with other children.

The difficulties that transcription presents for children mean that a good deal of attention comes to be focused on it. This is natural but can be counter-productive, especially if it means that composition receives less attention.

Progress and development in writing

Progress and development in writing will therefore be *multi-dimensional*. Some kinds of progress will be progress in the area of composition, and other kinds will relate mainly to transcription. In the primary years children's writing should show:

compositional aspects
– increasing control of story form
– increasing confidence and development of a 'voice' as a writer
– increasing awareness of audience and a developing sense of a reader and a reader's needs
– increasing familiarity with written language structures, and growing ability to make own writing explicit
– a widening range of forms, from early story forms and personal writing, to later more complex narrative and non-narrative forms
– increasing ability to manage extended texts

transcriptional aspects
– increasing control of standard spelling
– increasing ability to punctuate and lay out a text
– better control of handwriting and the development of a personal style

B3 Writing
Please comment on the child's progress and development as a writer in English and/or other community languages: the degree of confidence and independence as a writer; the range, quantity and variety of writing in all areas of the curriculum; the child's pleasure and involvement in writing both narrative and non-narrative, alone and in collaboration with others; the influence of reading on the child's writing; growing understanding of written language, its conventions and spelling.

L's composition is mature, confident and imaginative. He has a good sense of literary style and of the dramatic. He has written some interesting poems and historical stories. His spelling is not perfect but he has a good grasp of sentence construction. He shows a developing interest in writing.

What experiences and teaching have helped/would help development in this area? Record outcomes of any discussion with head teacher, other staff, or parents.

L. is now at a stage where greater emphasis could and should be placed upon his skills at transcription as he has a very sound and confident grasp of composition.

Bilingual writers

Bilingual children may well be developing as readers and writers in their first languages and, given the opportunity, can use this developing competence in the mainstream classroom. The child writing partly in one language and partly in the other is one obvious possibility, but some children may also wish to write at length in their first language, without necessarily recasting the writing into English. This kind of activity is valuable in itself, but is also useful as a way of increasing a child's awareness of the similiarities and differences between different language systems. Thought needs to be given to the fact that children writing in community languages will need some response to their writing, and the possibility of sharing it with an audience.

It is important that children feel that their first language is valued in the classroom and that they can make choices about the language they write in.

When recording bilingual children's progress in writing in English, it will be important to note the length of time they have been learning English.

Purposes for writing

In recent years the importance of real purposes for writing, and also of real audiences, has begun to be much more generally acknowledged. Many schools have seen the value of displaying and publishing children's work and of making it part of the school reading programme. Writing workshop approaches which offer children the opportunity to choose their own topics have helped to create a better climate for writing.

The school curriculum offers an amazingly broad range of opportunities for using writing for learning — from recording scientific observations in a log, to producing a finished information book for the school library. Some of the forms of 'writing across the curriculum' that might find a place in theme and topic work are:

– making lists (e.g. of things the class want to find out about tadpoles)

– note-taking (e.g. when interviewing a local resident about the history of the area)

◀ L *3rd year juniors — boy*
*Languages: **English***

The teacher has looked at every aspect of this boy's writing — his confidence and enjoyment in writing, his sense of written language, his skills as a writer, and his very considerable range.

B3

B3 Writing
Please comment on the child's progress and development as a writer in English and/or other community languages: the degree of confidence and independence as a writer; the range, quantity and variety of writing in all areas of the curriculum; the child's pleasure and involvement in writing both narrative and non-narrative, alone and in collaboration with others; the influence of reading on the child's writing; growing understanding of written language, its conventions and spelling.

S's writing is much more fluent in Bengali than in English at present. He has a good working knowledge of Bengali spelling system and shows a well-developed sense of narrative. He has enjoyed producing bi-lingual texts. He has also written simple reports and instructions in both languages and his English writing has developed in fluency and style. He's happy to have a go at unfamiliar words and tries quite hard to express himself on paper. He uses phonics quite heavily as an aid to spelling.

What experiences and teaching have helped/would help development in this area? Record outcomes of any discussion with head teacher, other staff, or parents.

Continued bi-lingual work, discussed with Bengali speaker to extend his written Bengali further.
Work on visual spelling patterns, introduce punctuation.
Real reasons for communicating on paper both in English and Bengali.

In this record the teacher has noted progress in both the languages that S. can write — English and Bengali, drawing on her own observations and those of the bilingual development/community language teacher. She comments on the range of his writing, his sense of form, his growing confidence, and his knowledge of the spelling system, and uses the second part of the section to make some detailed plans for helping S. to extend his writing.

'... the range, quantity and variety of writing in all areas of the curriculum...'

Children's writing grows more varied as they come to use it:

– for different *purposes*
– to express different *meanings*
– for different *audiences*

The earliest kinds of written language they use are likely to be personal *expressive* writing (writing close to everyday speech) and *poetic* writing (story and poetry). Factual ('*transactional*') writing will be developing too, but factual *narratives* (accounts, reports) are likely to be easier for children to handle than *non-narrative* factual writing. The range of one ten-year-old girl's writing over six months is shown below:

Account of experiment on lung capacity	'Rain' poem	Long space story (5 chapters)
Account of experiment on pulse rate	'Heart and Blood' poem	Story for young children
'The brain' (expository prose)	'Rain' poem in Bengali	

This shows a good range of kinds of writing with a strong emphasis on narrative (both factual and fictional). The curricular range is not so wide; most of the writing is science-based because the class had been engaged in a long piece of topic work on the human body. Teachers might like to use the matrix in the 'Talking and listening: diary of observations' to help them in analysing the range of children's writing in relation to the curriculum.

'... the child's pleasure and involvement in writing...'

Unless children are actively involved in their writing they are unlikely to develop rapidly as writers. They need to have strong purposes in order to carry them through some of the work they will have to face in undertaking an extended

---

– keeping journals/logs (e.g. 'learning logs' where children assemble information on a topic and formulate questions about the material)

– preparing a report (e.g. a report to the class on a group investigation)

– writing a script (e.g. for a taped documentary on alternative forms of energy)

– making a newspaper or magazine

– preparing a speech (for a formal class discussion)

– writing letters (e.g. exchanges with schools in other parts of the country or abroad; letters that are part of a piece of topic work)

– writing instructions (e.g. a handbook for the word-processor)

– using writing in combination with diagrams, charts and other models in order to record and communicate information effectively

– writing in role (e.g. as part of a drama project in history)

As well as being a means of learning, writing can also be a satisfaction in itself. The pleasure that comes from having made a good poem is close to the pleasure involved in other forms of making, such as painting or crafts.

Children who, in their writing, have something that it matters for them to say, or something that they very much want to make, are writers with genuine purposes. Development in writing really depends on the writer feeling this sort of involvement in the activity.

Some explanations of terms used in the 'Writing' section

'the degree of confidence and independence as a writer'

Children's confidence in writing, as in other areas of life, will obviously be affected by the attitudes of others, and especially by the way their writing is received and read. With encouragement, children can begin to be independent as writers from early on. It will be important however to gauge how much support they still need, and how far support can be withdrawn without throwing children entirely on their own resources. Gradually children should be able to take over more of the writing process for themselves, and to rely less on the teacher and more on their own knowledge and experience. Later the habit of taking responsibility for many aspects of their writing – from choosing their own subjects, to self-checking and editing – will encourage a mature approach to writing and to using writing as a means of learning.

piece of writing. 'Writing workshop' approaches put a lot of emphasis on children choosing their own topics for this reason. And once a child has completed a piece of writing, their pleasure in what they have done can be increased by the knowledge that it will be read by real readers.

'. . . both narrative and non-narrative . . .'

The chronological nature of *narrative*, and the fact that it is a kind of writing close to the ordering of speech, means that it is usually much easier for children to handle than *non-narrative* (description, argument) which has to be more deliberately organised. Young children can begin to understand non-narrative forms by using lists, matrices, and other ways of organising their knowledge. By the end of the primary school children should be beginning to tackle non-narrative writing more confidently.

'. . . alone and in collaboration with others . . .'

Although writing is thought of as an individual activity, collaboration is often a valuable way of using writing for learning. It can be particularly helpful for children to work together on information writing, which may initially be harder than story-writing. Collaboration can take many forms, from editing groups, to groups set up to read and respond to each others' writing, as well as collaborative writing projects.

'. . . the influence of reading on the child's writing . . .'

Children who are hearing stories read aloud frequently, or who are reading widely themselves, are absorbing the 'shapes' and 'tunes' of written language and learning to use them in their own compositions. (Because we generally introduce them to stories before anything else, the tunes they learn are most likely to be the tunes of fictional prose.) Often a child who has been reading a great deal of a particular author will take on their style and write in it for some time, like someone trying on another person's shoes.

'. . . growing understanding of written language . . .'

'Written language has to be more explicit than speech because it stands alone.'
K. Perera

Children's growing ability to make their own written language more explicit will develop as they become more conscious of their readers and as their sense of the patterns of written language is fed by their reading.

'. . . its conventions . . .'

This phrase covers features of the 'transcription' aspect of writing, and the layout of a text. Throughout the primary school children are

learning to use punctuation to 'mark' the meanings in their writing for their reader, to make their texts more coherent, and to add colour and expression. They learn these skills most effectively in real contexts. The main task young writers have in this area is knowing when to mark closure. Many children write in sentences but do not mark them with full stops. This, like the common problem of joining ideas together, and the repeated use of 'and', is part of the job of managing an extended text.

'. . . and spelling . . .'

The question of 'learning to spell' is particularly pressing in English, because of the irregular nature of the spelling system. For this reason a special section of 'Spelling in English' has been included here.

Spelling in English

The English spelling system is one of the most complicated systems there is, and for this reason it seems important to include a special note on learning to spell in English. The main reason why English presents such problems to a learner is because for a variety of historical reasons it is not a phonetically regular language – the sounds of the words do not offer a reliable guide to their spelling. This means that writers must rely on visual memory rather than on the sounds of words for help with spelling. It has been shown by Margaret Peters that good spellers generally do have a good visual memory.

Children are likely, therefore, to need to be shown effective strategies for improving their spelling. Though some children 'catch' spelling through their reading, most will need some teaching in this area. The most helpful teaching approaches will not rely on rules (which are unreliable) or on ready-made word lists (which are often ineffective) but will encourage children to attend to the appearance of words and to common letter sequences and to become good self-checkers.

Though too heavy an emphasis on spelling can be very inhibiting, too little attention to it can deprive children of important strategies, affect their confidence and also limit their writing. So considerable sensitivity is needed in deciding how and when to intervene. Short amounts of time given regularly to some kind of word study (e.g. study of word 'families' and roots) and to activities involving spelling is one way of providing indirect support, while individual children will also need help in looking at their own spellings and working out routes for improving them. The editing and 'publication' of children's work in the classroom offers a good context for children to proof-read their spellings, and for the production of a final draft that is error-free.

Teachers will need to adopt different approaches to spelling at different stages of the primary school, and the teachers of the youngest children will particularly want to consider the place of learning to spell in learning to write.

Very young children discovering the writing system

The youngest children in the nursery class or in reception infants, when they are writing independently, will be testing out their theories about how writing systems work (they may, of course, have experience of more than one system). They may also be exploring differences between drawing and writing, and focusing on features of print that they recognise (such as the letters in their name). They may not yet have realised how written symbols relate to spoken language, or to what is read aloud. Their 'writing' is likely to be an imitation of the appearance of print or script; they will often produce writing-like drawings, letter-like forms, or strings of letters and symbols but will not remember what they have written. Directionality may not be established.

Earliest attempts at spelling

Children who have begun to understand how language is written down will be using their understandings when they write independently. They will be developing ways of representing words and will be influenced in this by their experiences, the approaches to reading in use in their classroom, and the kinds of writing/spelling strategies they are encouraged to use by teachers. They may represent words *mainly* by what they can hear of them (e.g. initial sounds, clusters of consonants) and may indicate a syllable or a whole word by one letter. Children may also be developing visual strategies for spelling (especially when encouraged by their teachers) and be

attending to the words they see around them, remembering the shapes or words and finding spelling from books.

Approximating to standard spellings

As children gain in confidence as writers they will be more prepared to 'have a go' at spelling they do not know, without depending on teachers for the spelling of every word – and they will need to do this if they are to write at any length. Their invented spellings will often be logical and self-consistent, good guesses even if they are not absolutely correct. Their invented spellings are

likely to approximate more and more closely to standard spellings over time, but this will depend on their reading, their visual awareness, and the concepts they hold about the spelling system. At this stage it will be important to encourage them to use visual strategies more consistently, and to focus on the shapes and structures of words and on letter sequences. They may be able to check over their own writing for spellings they are not sure of, alone or with a partner, and to make collections of words they need to remember. Poetry, word play and word study will help to develop a sensitivity to words and to the relationships between them.

It will be a matter of concern if children continue to rely mainly on the sound of words as a guide to their spelling much beyond the middle infants, and they should not be encouraged to 'sound words out' as this is likely to mislead them. Handwriting will affect spelling; children who form letters consistently and write clearly and fluently are more likely to be good spellers.

Spelling caught *and* taught

After this, spelling development will depend partly on the child 'catching' standard forms of spelling, through reading, using and noticing words, and partly on the routines for teaching and learning spelling that are set up in classrooms. Children who are not naturally good spellers can be greatly helped by listing spellings they find problematic and using the 'look, cover, write, check' routine. It is useful if classroom routines encourage children to work together when checking for spelling; children can also pair up or work in very small groups when editing their own texts.

Where children are making multiple errors, teachers will find it useful to look at the errors with an analytic eye and try to perceive patterns of the error; this will provide a basis for working systematically with children, and make the whole business much more manageable for both child and teacher.

Part C is an important section because

(1) it enables the parent or parents to contribute their own feelings and judgements about the child's work and progress over the year, and to comment on the record after they have read it. Parents may be invited to add their comments at any time during the summer term, but may be particularly interested in reading Part B soon after it is completed.

(2) it gives another opportunity for inviting the child to comment on her/his progress. This second language and literacy conference offers the possibility of looking back over the year and recording the child's own assessment of her/his work.

(3) it gives an opportunity to record a final assessment of a child's progress over the last few months of the school year in all aspects of language and literacy. This ensures that the receiving teacher will have up-to-date information about the child's development.

(4) it allows teachers to pass on their experience and understanding of working with the child to her/his next teacher, and to make suggestions about the kind of support they think the child needs.

The section should be completed during the Summer Term (by half-term in the case of fourth-year juniors) and signed by the parent(s), class teacher and the headteacher of the school.

▶ Part C of D's completed record

Part C To be completed during the Summer Term*

C1 Comments on the record by child's parent(s) Reading has improved a great deal. His biggest thrill is being able to read to his sister – she still has to tell him a couple of words now and again but he's delighted that he can read well enough for her to listen. His spelling is getting better and he's interested in it now.

C2 Record of language/literacy conference with child
"Sometimes I need help when I'm reading when I don't understand a word. I enjoy reading best when I'm in bed because you can concentrate and when I read stories to my sister. I like reading in school but only when it's quiet, not when people come and annoy me. The bit of writing I like best is when I did it with S. – we had the same title, we decided it together, then we went away and wrote our own stories. When we read each others we both had Ghostbusters in it. Because S. writes fast he finished before me but then he had to go through it and put in commas and full-stops, but I do it slowly and do them as I go along and it takes a long time."

C3 Information for receiving teacher
This section is to ensure that information for the receiving teacher is as up to date as possible. Please comment on changes and development in any aspect of the child's language since Part B was completed.

D. has begun to view reading as a rewarding, satisfying thing 'to do' I think this has come from him being able to select his own reading material which he enjoys doing. In the last few weeks he has really come to grips with the fact that writing can be interesting and fun and has worked really well. He works very well in small groups. He has become a moderately fluent reader on reading scale 1.

What experiences and teaching have helped/would help development? Record outcomes of any discussion with head teacher, other staff, or parent(s).

It could be helpful to him if he didn't <u>always</u> play safe in his choice of books so maybe encourage him to select a wide range of reading material. After talking to D's mother we both agreed that he would enjoy and benefit from writing his stories on the computer as it may make it easier to get his thoughts onto paper more quickly.

Signed: Parent(s) _____   Class Teacher _____

Date _____   Head Teacher _____

*To be completed by the Summer half-term for 4th year juniors.

OBSERVATIONS AND SAMPLES

PRIMARY LANGUAGE RECORD

The observation and sample sheet is an optional element in the Primary Language Record. It offers a framework for teachers' observations of children's development in language and literacy. Observations recorded in this way can be drawn on when teachers are completing the main Primary Language Record, particularly Part B.

The observation and sample sheet is designed to be used alongside, or as part of, teachers' own records, and provides a means of making interim notes about children's language progress. It also identifies significant aspects of language growth to focus on, and sets out a structured way of looking.

There are four parts to the observation/sample sheet:
1. Talking and listening: diary of observations
2. Reading and Writing: diary of observations
3. Reading samples
4. Writing samples

The first two parts offer a simple open format for recording observations of significant points in a child's language and literacy development while the third and fourth parts provide formats for looking in depth at particular examples of a child's reading and writing.

Exact timings for the observations and samples are not suggested, but some recording would need to take place at least once or twice a term in order to build up a good continuous picture of development. Teachers who decide to integrate these records more firmly into their own systems may wish to use them much more

frequently, and the sheets can be freely copied by ILEA schools.

Some schools have chosen to take the headings from (for example) the reading sample sheet, and to use them in conjunction with their own much fuller recording systems, thus allowing children's reading to be sampled once a week or more. Teachers may feel that some children's language progress needs detailed recording, and decide to use the observation and sample sheets more frequently for these individuals. By the time teachers come to fill in Part B of the main Primary Language Record, they should have detailed evidence in the observation and sample sheets to support their general analysis of the child's progress.

There are all kinds of ways of adapting the observation and sample sheet to meet particular needs or fit into existing record systems. It is meant to be a tool for teachers, a means of facilitating observation, and should be used flexibly, in whatever way best suits a school's approach to recording. Some schools might choose to add further information to the observation and sample sheet, or to make it part of the day-to-day recording of other aspects of development, such as development in mathematics.

One element which is omitted from the Primary Language Record, but which most schools will probably want to add to it, is a list of the books a child has been reading. Children can begin to compile their own reading record from an early stage, and if a complete list proves too cumbersome to include, then children can be

involved in the selection of a list which will illustrate the range of their reading in a school year.

Storage of these kinds of records in the classroom, especially where examples of children's work are being kept, sometimes presents practical problems. Many teachers have come up with helpful solutions for organising and storing records in the classroom and these practical suggestions are fully described and illustrated in the appendix on storage and organisation (Appendix A).

Unlike the Primary Language Record, the observation and sample sheet is not intended to be passed on from teacher to teacher (unless of course this seems useful to the school). Its status is *informal*, and its function is to help teachers in their observations and informal assessments. A growing number of schools now use cumulative records of this kind, which keep careful track of children's progress in the rapidly developing primary years, and some of these informal records have provided models for the observation and sample sheet.

Many teaching decisions rest on detailed knowledge of children's individual learning paths, and on teachers' judgements of their progress. It is hoped that the frameworks presented in this part of the Primary Language Record will help teachers in formulating their observations, and will provide a convenient way of keeping track of individual progress.

1 Talking and listening: diary of observations

The space on this page of the observation and sample sheet is to be used for making diary-like entries about the talking that a child does with you or other children (and perhaps alone when the child is very young). If some aspects of a child's spoken language development can be recorded two or three times a term, by the end of the Spring Term teachers will have diary entries to refer to (as well as remembered examples) when recording conclusions about the child's progress on the Primary Language Record. The entries you make can be brief notes, or anecdotes about the child's talking with some detail of the context and who s/he was talking to. If you number and date your entries, you could record the same number on the matrix at the top of the page, which would give you an easy way of checking when, in what contexts and with whom the child was talking.

The two axes of the matrix reflect the two important dimensions of talking and listening that were discussed in some detail on page 19, and are a reminder of the range of possible contexts that a child might be observed working in.

Social contexts

Who we are talking to affects our confidence and sometimes the actual language we use. Talking with someone of a perceived higher status can be more difficult than talking to friends and equals. Thus for most children talking with an adult, even a known adult, can be more inhibiting than talking with another child. Therefore it is important that children should be observed interacting within different social situations. The

---

Observations and Samples (Primary Language Record)

attach extra pages where needed

Name: C.W. **Year Group:** Nursery

1 Talking & listening: diary of observations

The diary below is for recording examples of the child's developing use of talk for learning and for interacting with others in English and/or other community languages.

Include different kinds of talk (e.g. planning an event, solving a problem, expressing a point of view or feelings, reporting on the results of an investigation, telling a story . . .)

Note the child's experience and confidence in handling social dimensions of talk (e.g. initiating a discussion, listening to another contribution, qualifying former ideas, encouraging others . . .)

The matrix sets out some possible contexts for observing talk and listening. Observations made in the diary can be plotted on the matrix to record the range of social and curriculum contexts sampled: see notes pages 37-39

LEARNING CONTEXTS	pair	small group	child with adult	small/large group with adult
collaborative reading and writing activities				
play, dramatic play, drama & storying		Summer Term		
environmental studies & historical research				
maths & science investigations	December Lotto game			
design, construction, craft & art projects				
	informal context		September	

Dates	Observations and their contexts
Summer Term	First spontaneous verbal response other than yes or no. With other Nursery children in meadow. Is watching other children coming down the slide. Gets excited by this. Doesn't join in himself physically but becomes very involved in their play and enjoyment. Stands at the bottom of the slide shouting over and over again in a very loud voice " 1 - 2 - 3 - Go ! "
Sept. '86	Comes up to me and holds his foot up to me (shoelace is undone). Says nothing. When asked what he wants me to do, says, "Shoe." "Do you want me to do your shoelace up?" Replies "Yes." Similarly he would just say, "Water!" But now with encouragement (sometimes needed) he'll say, "Can I have some water, please."
Dec. '86	Playing picture lotto game with friend G.L. Quite a lot of conversation came out of this game. G.L. I've got two CW. I've got three G.L. You've got. I've got. CW. Yes. M. Who's got that one? G.L. There it is. I got no that. You've got it, that one. What that, Maureen? CW. Don't know. G.L. Who got that? C.W. Not he got it. No! G.L. I've got no shoe. I've got no socks. L. I want to play. G.L. You have to wait. C.W. I've got a car. Yes. Yes. No. He. I don't know that. Look Thomas (tank engine). Who's got this?

© ILEA

Observations and Samples (Primary Language Record)

attach extra pages where needed

Name: L **Year Group:** Top Junior

1 Talking & listening: diary of observations

The diary below is for recording examples of the child's developing use of talk for learning and for interacting with others in English and/or other community languages.

Include different kinds of talk (e.g. planning an event, solving a problem, expressing a point of view or feelings, reporting on the results of an investigation, telling a story . . .)

Note the child's experience and confidence in handling social dimensions of talk (e.g. initiating a discussion, listening to another contribution, qualifying former ideas, encouraging others . . .)

The matrix sets out some possible contexts for observing talk and listening. Observations made in the diary can be plotted on the matrix to record the range of social and curriculum contexts sampled: see notes pages 37-39

LEARNING CONTEXTS	pair	small group	child with adult	small/large group with adult
collaborative reading and writing activities			Feb.	
play, dramatic play, drama & storying				
environmental studies & historical research				March
maths & science investigations				
design, construction, craft & art projects				
dance and P.E.		Jan		

Dates	Observations and their contexts
1987 Jan.	In a group working in the gym (a collaborative group with peers) Very aware of others in group, quickly involved in discussion of the correct way of doing a movement, very forthcoming, explaining her ideas well to others in the group. Didn't listen so well to ideas from peers. However, did try out their suggestions — a very caring attitude, quiet concerned that a younger child didn't grasp my meaning. — took it upon herself to explain in words much simpler and with actions. Related well and the child happily followed L's explanation.
Feb.	In individual conversation with teacher re: silent reading. A very relaxed confident session. L chatted freely explaining why and how she chose her books — clear logical explanations, a trifle "wordy" in her conversation, but expresses herself well. Not afraid to make suggestions as to how we / the staff could make "book selection" easier for the children. Ideas such as group the books in "length of books", "size of print", number of pictures.
March.	In group with teacher. Tries to dominate conversation a bit by talking louder and more quickly....

© ILEA

CW *Nursery — boy*
Languages: **Cantonese, English**

These diary entries provided the evidence for the record on page 19. The teacher has entered what she saw as particularly interesting changes in CW's social and linguistic interactions with other children and with her. Some clear evidence in the December entry of his early learning of English by echoing his friend.

L *Top junior — girl*
Languages: **English**

Entries which reveal how L. is learning how to interact with other children: she enjoys explaining her ideas, but seems sometimes less ready to listen to others. She talks with confidence to her teacher and is conscious of what would help her as a learner. This is helpful evidence of the way that contexts will affect children's performance as talkers.

LEARNING CONTEXTS	SOCIAL CONTEXTS				
	pair	small group	child with adult	small/large group with adult	
collaborative reading and writing activities					
play, dramatic play, drama & storying					
environmental studies & historical research					
maths & science investigations					
design, construction, craft & art projects					

school are already sophisticated at handling many social dimensions of talk, and these can be built on as they progress through the school. You will be looking for the degree of confidence they show in a range of different situations in expressing their ideas and feelings. The child's personality will influence this and so will relationships with others in the group or pair, and understanding of and involvement in the topic, subject matter or ideas being talked about.

Some children may need more support than others in contributing through talk to the work of the classroom. Here, thinking about the size and composition of the groups and providing models for ways of working in groups would be helpful:

- teachers working *with* groups for short periods of time
- choosing children experienced at working in groups to work with those who are less experienced
- starting with pairs rather than groups

Children will take time to learn how to work effectively in groups. Group work is likely to be more successful in classrooms where collaboration and cooperation is felt to be more important than competition.

Alongside this it will be important to think about learning contexts in the classroom and how some of these can be organised so that they offer the opportunities children need for learning to work together and for exploring ideas through talk.

ones suggested on the horizontal axes are: as a member of a pair, in a small group, alone with an adult, or in a small or large group with an adult. There is an empty box if your observation does not fit these suggested contexts. An obvious addition for teachers working with very young children might be 'alone' since they often explore and play with spoken language through monologues, when involved in activities on their own.

You might also want to give more detail about the other members of a group a child is working with. Are they friends? Are they new to working together, or are they established in their working relationships? Is it a mixed group of boys and girls or a single sex group? Do they speak the same first language, or different? Are they interacting through English or other first languages?

It may also be important to look at the role of the adult in the small group. Is the adult working as a member of the group, or as an observer or leader of the group? Does s/he speak the same first language as the children or some of the children?

These kinds of differences can affect the

dynamic of the interaction in a group or between pairs; they can be particularly significant in classrooms that are culturally and linguistically mixed, where for example, any antagonism to children because of race or colour or languages spoken can crucially affect their confidence in themselves as communicators. Observations of children at work will inform you, not only of a particular children's spoken language development, but also about the cultural interaction of the classroom.

Suggestions of the kinds of things you would be looking for in the social dimensions of talk can be seen in the short note next to the matrix:

Note the child's experience and confidence in handling social dimensions of talk (e.g. initiating a discussion, listening to another's contribution, qualifying former ideas, encouraging others. . .)

This list is not meant to be exhaustive. Other possibilities could be included, asking questions about the way things work, putting forward new ideas, defending ideas, framing statements for a particular audience. . . .

Most young children when they come to

Learning contexts

Potentially all areas of the curriculum provide contexts for children to explore and extend their use of spoken language. And it is crucial to organise the learning contexts of the classroom so as to give a wide range of opportunities for language development. *Some* kinds of talk will come from children working collaboratively in small groups, using their language to further their understanding of the learning task in hand. *Other* kinds of talk will be needed in sharing with a large group or the whole class what has been learned in the smaller groups.

Small groups provide safe environments for exploring ideas and materials often in quite tentative ways. They also allow for close working relationships between members of the group. Large groups have another function and make different demands on children's talk, with a greater need for making what is being said explicit and clear for those who have not been involved in the work of the small group. Children as they move through the primary school need experience of using their language in both small and large groups.

Some of the curriculum contexts that offer children opportunities for exploring their use of language are listed on the vertical axis of the matrix, with empty boxes for you to add to if you wish.

Collaborative reading and writing activities

Although they are described separately, reading, writing and talking are closely linked and feed each other. In developing their spoken language children will be learning from their writing and their reading, as well as drawing on conversations with other children and adults.

Also many of the reading and writing activities that children are engaged in will involve them in working collaboratively, so that talk and discussion will be important elements – for example, writing stories together, preparing an account of a science investigation, recording the results of a maths activity, making a pie chart, plotting a journey....

Some of the aspects of talk you could be looking for are these:

- the influence of children's reading on their talk – words or phrases from stories or texts that children have read appearing in their spoken repertoire

- children's interpretations of the language of books and of word meanings

- children's appreciation of different styles in both spoken and written language, and their sense of the differences between spoken and written language

- children's appreciation of subtle nuances of words (e.g. when reading or writing poetry)

- children's ability to identify and discuss ideas that are present in a text or a story

- children's ability to contribute positively to a group process (e.g. when writing collaboratively) and to make helpful suggestions

Play, dramatic play, drama

Young children use their play to explore new experiences and to relate them to earlier understandings. Through play they express their thoughts and feelings and develop their imagination. They talk as they play – to themselves and to each other. A classroom environment that encourages dramatic play and spontaneous role-play will also encourage children's talk.

Role-play and improvisation can create opportunities for observing children in a context for talk that will reveal not only a child's ear for dialogue and dialect, but also her/his understanding of the issues s/he is exploring. In role-play children can explore an issue from within a framework that may be different from their own, and can find ways of interacting with others through the role.

By entering into the framework *with* children we can encourage them to explore different ways of responding to situations and sometimes challenge their thinking.

Some of the aspects of talk you could look for are these:

- children speaking in the language of the roles they are playing

- their awareness of differences in contexts and how they change their dialect, accent, and style for different contexts

- their ability to sustain a flow of language during play and role-play

- confidence in handling and presenting arguments and ideas while in role

- children exploring roles and issues in community languages

Storying

Most children will have a fund of stories they have been told or have had read to them. When they come to school they will already know about the shapes stories can take, and be familiar with much story language – through English or other community languages. Many children will already be skilled story-tellers, telling stories to themselves or for others to listen to. Some children will need encouragement to do that.

Look for all the ways that children are playing with language, extending and pushing to the limits what they already know, inventing new ways of saying things and creating elaborate plots and imagined situations.

Curriculum areas

These all offer opportunities for a range of similar kinds of talk, depending on the kind of activity that children are involved in and how the working group is organised:

making plans, for example, for a maths survey, for the construction of a model, for investigating goods sold in shops in the neighbourhood...
reporting on the results of an investigation, the exploration of a problem...
describing how a model was made, the details of a journey...
anticipating what might happen if particular materials were used, or what might be seen

at the museum, or if paper parachutes were made bigger...

Sometimes there will be sustained discussion during an activity or an investigation. Sometimes this will follow afterwards in reporting on what has happened or which ideas were explored.

There should also be opportunities for watching interaction between children, and observing, for example, how ideas are explored and sustained through a group discussion, and the role that each child plays.

The teacher's role

Some of these observations will involve you in interaction with individual children or groups, particularly when you are wanting to encourage children to tell you about something they have done or are interested in. Then you will be both part of the interaction and observing it. Your opening moves or the kinds of questions you ask will be especially important here. The form of the questions you ask will affect the ways children can reply. Some questions only allow a one-word response, for example, 'Did that piece of wood sink in the water?' 'No.' 'Did you like that story?' 'Yes.'

These are called *closed questions*. Sometimes judgements about children's skill at talking and listening have been made on their responses to closed questions. What you want to aim for are *open-ended* questions, for example, 'Tell me what happened to that piece of wood in the water?' 'How do you think Titch felt in the story?' These allow children to make more thoughtful responses, and to inform you about what they have observed or how they are feeling.

2 Reading and Writing: diary of observations

This section is intended as a cumulative record of observations describing a child's development as a reader and a writer in the context of the classroom. Entries can be made several times each term, or more frequently, as part of a teacher's day-to-day record keeping. Additional sheets can be attached if required.

The recording of information in diary form continues the pattern set by the previous section and helps to link the child's development across the inter-related aspects of talking and listening, reading and writing. The diary invites the teacher to build up a picture of a child's reading and writing behaviour in different social and curriculum contexts in order to chart and promote development. The matrix in the 'talk' section may also provide a helpful framework for observation here.

To provide a close focus for observation, the section is divided into 'reading' and 'writing', but the important connections between the two are clear. Notes will include examples of a child's growing confidence, involvement and understanding as a reader and a writer in English and/or other community languages. Examples may show ways in which children's reading influences their writing or how their understanding of reading grows through the writing process.

Very young children generally come to school having learned something about reading and writing at home. It is important to include here examples of children's early reading and writing experiences and to observe the ways in which story features in their development as readers and writers.

As you record anecdotes and stories about a child's reading and writing over time, a picture of development emerges. Looking back on these cumulative observations you will be able to draw conclusions about significant developments a child makes and to see where support is needed.

This information, together the insights gained from the 'child conference' in particular, can provide a powerful means of supporting and extending a child's growth as an independent reader and writer, and will help when you come to complete Part B of the Primary Language Record.

Strategies for classroom observation

It is envisaged that these observations will be made in the course of daily classroom activities. Many teachers already note down a child's significant literacy developments as they arise and these are the kinds of comments to include in the diary. There are various ways of organising observations to ensure that entries are made regularly for each child. You may wish to focus on small groups of children working together on a specific activity, perhaps observing a different group each day. Alternatively you could follow one or two children during the course of a day, recording their reading and writing behaviour within a range of activities, for example, a science investigation, bookmaking, listening to a class story. Another way might be to select an area of the classroom in which to observe children, the book corner or the maths area, for example.

It might also be useful to sample how a child's reading has developed in relation to a particular book or to look at how a child's handling of story-writing has matured.

Talking to children about their work contributes to the observation process. It provides opportunities for children to reflect on their own learning and allows teacher and child to share their observations.

Reading observations

Reading in English and/or other community languages

Much of the reading experience at school will be in English, but for bilingual children literacy in their community language(s) needs to be encouraged and extended. This will involve creating an atmosphere in which language variety is seen positively, for example, through the provision of books and materials in languages other than English and the organising of support from bilingual colleagues and parents. Opportunities can be created for talking with children about books written in languages the teacher may not understand, and children who share a community language can sometimes be invited to read together in this language.

As some bilingual children may be more experienced readers in their community language(s) than in English, it is important to record this and to enable children to develop literacy in community language(s) across the curriculum.

Information sources in community languages can sometimes be provided and children can occasionally work in shared language groups for some activities, for example.

When observing bilingual children's development as readers of English it will be important to be aware of how long children have been learning English.

Record observations of the child's development as a reader (including wider experiences of story) across a range of contexts

It may be helpful to consider how the child behaves as a reader in relation to the following aspects of reading and kinds of classroom/curriculum contexts:

- how the child responds to books and the world of print
- how the child chooses and uses books and materials for different reading purposes
- what kinds of books/texts the child chooses to read and the range, variety and quantity of the child's reading across the curriculum
- how independent and confident the child is when reading
- whether the child gets involved in books/texts and sustains that involvement over time
- whether the child is willing to share and discuss books
- what experiences the child has of story and the conventions of stories (through story-telling, story-making, retelling stories, drama and discussion)
- whether the child can read critically (by questioning the text and reflecting on what has been read)

How the child responds to books and the world of print

For very young children this may involve recognising their names in books and on labels in the classroom, identifying letters or talking their way through a favourite story book such as *Rosie's Walk* or *The Old Woman and the Rice Thief*.

For others, signs that reading is experienced as an enjoyable and meaningful activity might include: choosing to read without adult persuasion, seeking texts in first and second languages, sharing joke books with friends, re-reading and re-telling favourite stories, recommending a 'good' book to another member of the class or using the computer for word-processing.

Children's interest in books and print grows from positive experiences.

For children who appear to be uninterested in reading, these kinds of experiences need to be provided and material made available to match individual interests and linguistic experience.

How the child chooses and uses books and materials for different reading purposes

A child may, for example, choose to read *Mr. Gumpy's Outing* because s/he is familiar with other books by John Burningham, either through reading them or hearing them read aloud. An older child might opt for a novel by Margaret Mahy or Rosa Guy after having seen a film or a TV programme, or following a recommendation from a friend.

By browsing through a book, reading the first few pages or the description on the cover before making a selection, a child demonstrates her/his growing autonomy as a reader.

Children read information books very differently at different times, depending on their purposes for consulting the book. They may, for example, read everything available on the subject of insects because they are pursuing a personal interest or they may need to use several sources and locate particular paragraphs when investigating the difference between butterflies and moths as part of their topic work.

Children can be encouraged to share the strategies they use for choosing books, learning from each other through small-group or paired discussions. Different approaches can also be highlighted by the teacher.

What kinds of books/texts the child chooses to read and the range, variety and quantity of the child's reading across the curriculum

In the same way that adults read at a variety of levels (from magazines to insurance forms to poetry) so children need opportunities to experience both texts that are demanding and those which provide reassurance.

A child who is beginning to tackle texts like *The Iron Man* by Ted Hughes may also need to relax with a favourite such as *Funnybones* by the Ahlbergs. Children who consistently choose books which are very familiar to them and do not extend their reading can be encouraged to try different material through reading with a partner, listening to taped stories or being given a book to take home which has been introduced to the class, for example.

As suggested earlier children might like to keep lists themselves, perhaps with their comments about the books they read. These records can be kept with the observation and sample sheets and discussed with the children, helping them to become more aware of their own reading patterns.

▶ J 3rd year junior — girl
Languages: **English**

In this series of observations there is evidence of the range and variety of J's reading which is supported by J's own record of the books she has read. The sample shows the strategies J. uses for choosing books, for example, selecting books from a favourite series or in connection with a class topic. There are also insights into the processes she engages in when reading and writing.

---

2 Reading and Writing: diary of observations
(reading and writing in English and/or other community languages)

Dates	Reading
	Record actual examples of the child's reading (including wider experiences of story) across a range of contexts.
Sept '87	Reading fluently and thoroughly enjoys reading fiction. Has just finished reading Silver Sword by I. Serraillier and is at the moment unable to pick up another book to read because, "I'll never be able to follow that, it was so brilliant and it's still in my head !"
Oct '87	Is reading a varied diet of authors. Keeps own record of books read at home / school and always makes valid comments which I'm able to discuss with her. Last year she got very hooked on L.I. Wilder series. Has read information books about the oak tree and woodland life in general and has taken some home to read and work from in connection with class centre of interest. Uses 'contents' / 'index' well.
Nov '87	Has dipped into the Wilder series once more — "I know these books. I can really feel a part of them." — the whole of the family is reading them. "I enjoy reading to myself. You can read quickly and sometimes I skip over words. I can be 2 people in a book." When J. reads aloud she cannot read quickly enough for herself — often chooses to read passages of favourite books to me - to her mum.

Writing
Record actual examples of the child's writing (including stories dictated by the child) across a range of contexts.

Dates	
Oct '87	Is an avid writer — can't stop! Takes notebook home every night to write down her thoughts mainly through poetry. Makes notes and writes thoughts often in wordswebs before beginning the actual poem. Reads and re-reads her work and is not afraid to cross out and to keep working on her writing until she is completely satisfied.
Nov. 87	Has been inspired to write many poems about the countryside after our week on school journey at Marchants Hill Rural Centre. Has now made her own poetry book containing all her poems written over the last two months. She is now able to write poems in the appropriate format. Her poetry is very lyrical. Have tried to introduce her to different poetic styles — she is reading Gargling with Jelly by B. Patten. Has produced good information writing about diseases of oak leaves using first and second source material - has maintained a strong personal style.

How independent and confident the child is when reading

A child's confidence and independence in reading will vary with the type of text being read and with the context. For example, a child may read *Peepo* with ease and confidence but experience difficulty with another apparently simple text because it is badly constructed and doesn't provide the reader with rhythms and natural patterns of language to tune into.

A child may read and use instructions in constructing a model but have difficulty in making sense of the same kind of material if it forms part of a comprehension exercise, divorced from a real context.

Another child may confidently share in reading Gail Haley's *A Story, A Story* with a partner, but be reluctant to tackle it alone.

Through having access to good quality texts (including story tapes and texts in community languages), real contexts for reading, shared

---

2 Reading and Writing: diary of observations
(reading and writing in English and/or other community languages)

Dates	Reading
	Record actual examples of the child's reading (including wider experiences of story) across a range of contexts.
13.1.87	Knows many rhymes & jingles from 'To Market' and 'Bibbili bonty' Storychest rhyme books. 'If I Had a Donkey' 'Mary lost her Coat' plus a number of playground rhymes. Often will choose 'big books', picture books as well as Storychest to read with 2 or 3 friends. Will often repeat catchphrases out of context, applying them to life experiences. When asked to leave an activity for a moment to do something else, she said, "If I look round I'll forget" — a refrain from a favourite book.
27.1.87	First thing in the morning, before the register is taken, A. sorts out the book she is going to read with a friend. Often chooses a book where there is more than one copy of the same.
4.2.87	A. read a shared-writing book 'The Paper-bag Princess' to a group of friends first thing this morning.

	Writing
	Record actual examples of the child's writing (including stories dictated by the child) across a range of contexts.
13.1.87	Wrote out shopping lists for a shopping activity in the classroom.
18.2.87	A's brother has just brought me a book he has written with the help of A. and their father, entitled 'Mrs. Tibbs & family', following the birth of kittens in their family!
March	A. made a poster for our home corner which had been made into a pet shop. She looked up words in a book on pets. Because this was a poster, she wanted the correct spelling & used her initiative to look them up. Has written own cat story over 2 sessions! Lots of story conventions.
April	
May	A. is writing an imaginative story on 'Noah's Ark' It is bright and colourful and has a beginning, middle and an end. (Topic on water)

A *Middle infant — girl*
*Languages: **English***

The child in this sample is encouraged to make choices about the kinds of books she reads and has opportunities to decide when to read and with whom. She has access to a wide range of material and applies understanding from her reading in other contexts. This can be seen in her writing, where she uses story conventions and is involved in different kinds of writing e.g. lists, stories, group books.

---

2 Reading and Writing: diary of observations
(reading and writing in English and/or other community languages)

Dates	Reading
	Record actual examples of the child's reading (including wider experiences of story) across a range of contexts.
1st week of term	K. shows little inclination to look at books when in the book corner. He enjoys conversation with other children at this time.
2.10.87	M. (K's cousin) read 'The Cat sat on the Mat' with him. K. became greatly excited, "Miss, can I read it to you?" He took the book home to read.
16.10.87	K. returned to 'Cat on the mat' after quite a long gap — asked me to listen to him reading it. Confidently recalled the story.
2.11.87	K. read a small caption which accompanied a drawing of a sycamore 'wing' on the nature table.
13.11.87	Browsing in the book corner he became excited by finding the smaller version of 'The Hungry Giant'. "It's the same as this book!" pointing to the 'big book'.
16.11.87	K. brought in 3 pages from a Hindi date calendar for our 'Home Writing' Board.

	Writing
	Record actual examples of the child's writing (including stories dictated by the child) across a range of contexts.
Sept.	K. tried to make his first book (other children were making some so he wanted to join in). Tried to write his name but became frustrated.
2.10.87	K. asked me to help him write his name. We talked about it and practised each letter. Finally managed a 'k'. He was delighted.
6.10.87	Father sent in a Hindi/English alphabet & put it on the noticeboard.
9.10.87	Big breakthrough — K. managed to copy his name today.
14.10.87	K's first attempts at 'independent writing'. "I'm going to write a story." Echoes of 'The Hungry Giant' Storychest story. Evidence of letters from his name in his writing.
15.10.87	K. suggested a notice for our bottle collection & dictated it to me. Drew a bottle to illustrate the notice.
16.10.87	Playing in the class shop 'Mr. Baker's Sandwich Bar' he took orders on the telephone & wrote on the jotter pad.

K *Reception — boy*
*Languages: **Hindi, English***

The teacher here has made frequent entries because she uses the diary as a day to day recording system in charting the rapid development of this bilingual child.

This sample shows how the child's interest in print, and confidence as a reader and a writer is developing in a variety of social settings and curriculum contexts. There are also important links made for the children between literacy at home and at school, for example in the ways the child's first language is valued in the classroom.

experiences of story, and opportunities for drama and story-telling activities, children can be supported in their development as independent and confident readers.

Whether the child gets involved in books/texts and sustains that involvement over time

Signs that a child is able to engage with texts in a sustained way might include occasions when an individual is absorbed in a book for a long time in the book corner or when a child's interest is held by a book over a period of days or even weeks.

You may notice a child's involvement with a particular book when s/he talks about it enthusiastically to other children and adults, or asks to take a book home immediately after you have finished reading it to the class.

When sharing a book, for example, Maurice Sendak's *Where the Wild Things Are*, a child may refer to other books s/he is reminded of by the story, or relate personal experiences of dreaming, or of being naughty, in trouble, or scared.

A child may return to a favourite book time and again, and it is worth recording the title and discovering the special meanings it has for the child. Children may also become involved in the work of a particular author and may want to read all the books by, for example, Paula Fox or Dick King-Smith.

Whether the child is willing to share and discuss books

Children often have reading partners with whom they share stories and texts or talk about their books. Two children reading *The Jolly Postman*, for example, show their understanding of the text by reading the various 'letters' in role and retelling the tales referred to in the book. They may decide to build on their understanding by creating their own version of the book, using their reading experience for developing their range as writers.

Older children may be prepared to share their enthusiasm for particular books (e.g. *The Never-Ending Story, A Thief in the Village*) with the rest of the class as part of a regular 'book programme'.

These observations are significant indicators of a child's growing awareness of the content and form of stories and texts, and their readiness to reflect on their reading.

It is also important to observe children reading across the curriculum, for example, a group following printed instructions in making an electrical circuit. You can note down the ways they refer to the text, re-read particular phrases and interpret diagrams, and see how far they are able to make good use of the text in constructing their circuit.

What experiences the child has of story and the conventions of stories

Story plays a central role in learning to read and is important for children of all ages in their literacy development. Many children come to school with a knowledge of story, from being read to at home or from listening to adults tell stories.

In the classroom you might observe the children building on this experience through listening to and joining in with stories told or read aloud and making up their own stories.

When a group of young children are listening to a traditional tale, many will join in with 'once upon a time' or offer alternative, conventional beginnings. They may recognise the story, respond to repetition or anticipate what happens next in the plot. Often they can identify the villain, the main character, the conventional use of three (eg. three wishes) and even enjoy the dangers, secure in the expectation of a happy ending.

Very young children may confidently 'read' books, creating stories by using the pictures or by modelling themselves on adults and retelling the story from memory. Stories like *Not Now Bernard* by David McKee are often memorised and retold with extraordinary animation and accuracy.

Children's awareness of songs and rhymes will also contribute to their growing enjoyment of language and its rhythms and patterns.

Indications that children are gaining wider experience of story may be that they recognise different kinds of stories and explore a variety of story-telling techniques. After reading *The Paper Bag Princess* for example, children might recast traditional tales with female main characters or invent contemporary fairy tales. They may take on complex narratives such as *Ghost Child* by Catherine Sefton, and show through role-play or discussion that they are beginning to recognise the different threads in the story and to make links between them in understanding the text and its structure.

Whether the child can read critically

Signs of an ability to read critically can be seen in the very young. For instance, when children listen to stories read aloud, they may question the reader, as they later learn to question the text, about events in the story, the way the characters behave and the outcomes of the plot. To test a story they may relate it to their own experience or ask 'if it's real'.

Indications of older children's growing critical awareness can be found in their comments on the detail of particular books, their sense that there is a writer at work and their discussion of a writer's ideas.

Models for this critical approach are often provided by adults and children's own curiosity can be directed in activities such as considering bias by examining images of women in a selection of books, or analysing the ways different newspapers report a story.

As children discuss what they read with other children and adults and write about their reading, critical evaluation and reflection can become part of their reading process.

Writing observations

Writing in English and/or other community languages

Bilingual children need opportunities in school to write in their community language(s) as well as in English. For this to happen, there needs to be a supportive classroom context where language variety is evident in the provision of books and materials, in displayed work and in the involvement of bilingual colleagues and parents.

Children can be invited to choose to write in their community language(s) or in English and encouraged to bring to school any writing they may have done at home or at their community school. Writing can be 'published' in school and made available to wider audiences of children or parents.

Occasionally, children sharing the same language can be grouped together for some activities to write and discuss their work using their first language. By encouraging bilingual children to talk about their writing, the ideas, the content and the way they went about the writing, a teacher who may not understand the language can become involved and give support to their developing biliteracy.

Record observations of the child's development as a writer (including stories dictated by the child) across a range of contexts.

It may be helpful to consider how the child behaves as a writer in relation to the following aspects of writing and types of classroom/curriculum contexts:

- the child's pleasure and interest in writing

- the range and variety of her/his writing across the curriculum

- how independent and confident the child is when writing

- whether the child gets involved in writing and sustains that involvement over time

- the child's willingness to write collaboratively and to share and discuss her/his writing

- the understanding the child has of written language conventions and the spelling system

The child's pleasure and interest in writing

For very young children this may involve playing at writing in the home corner (taking telephone messages, making shopping lists), choosing to write their own names again and again, dictating stories for an adult 'scribe', using writing to extend the meanings in their drawings and making books to read and show to others.

Children who are becoming more experienced as writers may indicate their interest in writing through keeping personal journals, writing letters regularly to family and friends, bringing to school stories and poems written at home, writing intently over a period of time and taking pleasure in sharing their work with others. They will often initiate writing activities, deciding to make a book, suggesting an idea for a story, choosing a form for a piece of writing or perhaps asking to take home a piece of written work to finish it.

The range and variety of the child's writing

Many young children can be observed writing for different purposes. They may be seen making lists, writing notes (perhaps to their parents about a class visit), sending greeting cards, making name labels or composing rhymes, songs and stories.

Bilingual children may, in addition, recognise and use written forms of English and their community language(s).

In observing a child who is growing more experienced as a writer, look for examples of the variety of writing s/he does across the curriculum; the kinds of stories (fairy tales, Anansi stories,

personal stories . . .), the range of poetry (haiku, free verse, serious, humorous poems . . .), and information writing (composing a questionnaire, annotating a diagram, planning and writing instructions or a report . . .).

How independent and confident the child is when writing

In making your observations you will need to take account of the context in which a child is working and note her/his purposes for writing as these factors will affect a child's confidence and independence.

A child may, for example, confidently write about losing her/his temper after reading and discussing *Angry Arthur* but find difficulty in doing so without a similarly supportive introduction. Some children will happily collaborate in writing a shared poem, but might initially avoid this kind of writing if expected to tackle it alone. Similarly, a child can be enabled to write independently by knowing that the writing is a first draft, but may be inhibited about writing a 'finished piece' at the first attempt.

It will be helpful to note down the resources a child makes use of in the course of their writing (e.g. other children, adults, word banks, books/texts), and how s/he decides on the form of presentation.

Whether the child gets involved in writing and sustains that involvement over time

Examples might include occasions when an individual is absorbed in composing a story alone or with others for a long time in the writing area or when s/he continues to add to and revise a piece of writing over a period of days, perhaps completing some of it at home.

You may be aware of the child's engagement with a particular piece of writing through her/his eagerness to discuss it, read it, present it in book form or make a story-tape. Children may also use the writing in their dramatic play or as part of an oral presentation (in an assembly, for a tape-slide show, for story-telling or dramatisation).

The child's willingness to write collaboratively and to share and discuss her/his writing

Children often have opportunities to work with partners with whom they can discuss their ideas for the writing, decide on the form of presentation, share the research, compose and edit. In the course of working together, two children will share what they know about the writing process as well as the subject, and this provides a useful context for observation.

Observing children composing a group

story, perhaps after reading a big book, can reveal valuable insights into the ways they operate within a group and the kinds of contributions they make to the shared writing. For example, a child working in this way might take on the role of editor, drawing the group's attention to parts of the text that 'don't make sense', and offering alternative suggestions.

The use the child makes of her/his experience of story and the conventions of stories in writing

Look for examples of children, in their earliest attempts at writing, composing stories about their own experience and creating their own versions of stories they know well. They may tell stories through writing and drawing, and will often be eager to read their compositions to others.

Many children are keen to tell their stories for an adult or another child to write down. By observing children dictating stories you can learn about the use they make of story language ('Long, long ago there lived . . .') and the story form, for example the use of recurring sequences.

As children develop as readers you might expect their writing to reflect, to some extent, the range and variety of stories they experience. A child may model a story on *A Dark, Dark Tale* for example, building suspense and creating a surprise ending of their own. They may be more aware of writing for different audiences, and learn to write stories for younger children as well as their peers, perhaps presenting them in book form. An older child may try on a favourite author's style for a time, and write like Michael Rosen or Betsy Byars.

The understanding the child has of written language conventions and the spelling system

Signs that young children are learning about written language conventions are likely to emerge through shared reading and writing activities. Where the teacher is using a 'big book' with a group for example, a child may ask about the inverted commas in the text and begin to use them in her/his own writing.

Also, by inviting children to read their writing aloud, you may get a sense of their understanding of how a text can be marked for punctuation and then help them to find ways of using full stops, for instance, to assist the reader.

In the context of a child's writing you can observe her/his growing understanding of the spelling system, noting examples of invented spelling and the other strategies they use such as trying out different spellings of words before choosing the 'best' version, consulting a dictionary and so on.

3 Reading samples

This section of the observation and sample sheet offers a framework for sampling a child's development when reading particular texts. This form of assessment can be used once a term or more frequently and if photocopied the sample sheet can become part of a teacher's day-to-day record system. The reading samples section provides three different procedures for looking at a child's progress and development in some depth and the procedure chosen will depend almost entirely on the child's expertise as a reader.

Reading samples: notes on headings

Reading in English and/or other community languages

All children will be reading or learning to read in English and many bilingual children will be reading in one or more community languages as well as English. Teachers in schools are actively engaged in encouraging children's biliteracy and it is crucial that this all-round development of a child is valued and supported. In some schools there will be classroom teachers who are bilingual; there may also be bilingual development/community language teachers who will be working on a regular basis with children in the classroom and they will be able to assess children's reading in languages other than English. If help of this kind is not available, classroom teachers can discover a great deal from listening to a child read aloud and from talking with them about what they are reading in another language (see page 58). Further help and advice can be sought from bilingual colleagues, or parents or older siblings. It is worth noting that learning to read in two languages will give children a well informed understanding of ways in which written language systems work. Being able to read in one language supports learning to read in another.

When assessing bilingual children's reading in English, it will be important to note how long they have been learning English.

This might include an element of silent reading (see page 25)

From the time that children become absorbed in revisiting familiar books, in re-enacting known texts, in reflecting on meanings and exploring possibilities, they are on the way to becoming silent readers. Therefore, when sampling children's reading, whether they are inexperienced or experienced readers, an appropriate amount of time can be given to each child to:

– look through a book/text in order to become familiar with it again or

– practise reading the text in preparation for reading aloud to the teacher, and/or

– read a substantial part of the text silently

This general procedure for sampling gives due weight to the importance of silent reading.

Title of book/text (fiction or information) and known text/unknown text

These entries will provide a developing picture of the range and variety of texts selected for sampling reading development and give insights into a child's growing confidence and competence as a reader. At the early stages of reading a child will be growing in confidence with a selected number of familiar books or stories. S/he will come to know these texts very well, often by heart. It is from watching and listening to a child read aloud these known texts that we can discover the kinds of reading strategies a child is using at this early stage.

As a reader becomes more experienced, more aware of print and of different kinds of texts s/he will be able to tackle a wider range and variety of unfamiliar and unknown books and reading material (fiction and information) with growing confidence.

It is important to remember that books carry cultural meanings, and that children may be able to take on some texts more confidently if they find a familiar world in them. So the book stock in a classroom should always contain stories from the different cultural traditions represented in a class (as well as others). It also needs to be recognised that books may be biased and negative, or even sexist or racist. Children are likely to be affected by these implicit messages. It is essential to try to ensure that the books available for children's reading are free of harmful prejudice or insulting images; these kinds of factors will need to be considered in choosing a text with a child.

Sampling procedure used: informal assessment/running record/miscue analysis

The rationale and procedural detail for each sampling procedure can be found in the appendices.

Informal Assessment – Appendix C (page 58)
Running Record – Appendix D (pages 59-61)
Miscue Analysis – Appendix E (pages 61-63)

This choice of sampling procedures offers three structured frameworks for assessing a child's reading progress. The *Running Record* is particularly appropriate for an inexperienced reader and focuses on a developing understanding of concepts of print. *Miscue Analysis*, for the more experienced but not yet fully independent reader, provides a clear picture of how far a child uses all the available reading strategies and cue systems to read and understand an unknown text. *Informal Assessment* is suitable for use with all children, whatever their age or experience; it provides a framework for looking at a reader's all-round development.

The discussion that accompanies and follows the reading (aloud and silently) will help teachers to gauge the nature and depth of a child's understanding of a text; it will also pave the way for planning subsequent reading experiences and taking any other action that might seem necessary to further development.

The diagrams below will be of assistance in helping teachers to choose a sampling procedure:

1 Overall impression of the child's reading

This is an opportunity to evaluate in general terms the ways in which the child responded to reading a particular book/text on this particular occasion:

– *confidence and degree of independence*

This would involve commenting on how the child approached the activity, how s/he managed the reading of the text and whether or not s/he relied heavily on the teacher for support.

– *involvement in the book/text*

Noticing how engaged the child was in the book/text how long s/he spent in browsing or reading and how s/he responded generally to the reading experience.

– *the way in which the child read the text aloud*

So much can be deduced about a child as a reader, when s/he reads aloud (whether in English or another language) e.g. how much s/he enjoyed the book/text and reading it aloud, whether or not s/he read in large meaningful chunks of language, the pace at which s/he read, and the use of intonation to convey understanding and feeling.

2 Strategies the child used when reading aloud (see page 24)

NB The tinted 'band' identifies clearly those strategies which indicate that a young child is beginning to take on some important aspects of reading. These are further identified by asterisks that relate to a footnote ("early indicators that a child is moving into reading").

In general, teachers of young inexperienced readers will refer mainly to the strategies within the band, while teachers of more experienced readers will refer to strategies outside the band. The first item in the strategies section ("drawing on previous experience to make sense of the book/text") can obviously apply to readers at any stage.

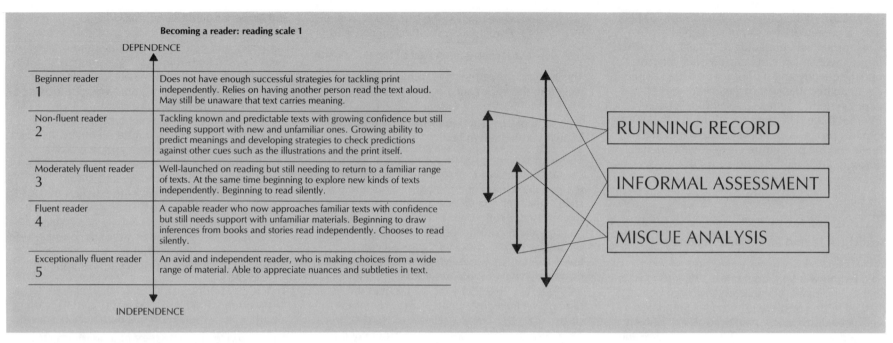

Becoming a reader: reading scale 1

DEPENDENCE

Beginner reader 1	Does not have enough successful strategies for tackling print independently. Relies on having another person read the text aloud. May still be unaware that text carries meaning.
Non-fluent reader 2	Tackling known and predictable texts with growing confidence but still needing support with new and unfamiliar ones. Growing ability to predict meanings and developing strategies to check predictions against other cues such as the illustrations and the print itself.
Moderately fluent reader 3	Well-launched on reading but still needing to return to a familiar range of texts. At the same time beginning to explore new kinds of texts independently. Beginning to read silently.
Fluent reader 4	A capable reader who now approaches familiar texts with confidence but still needs support with unfamiliar materials. Beginning to draw inferences from books and stories read independently. Chooses to read silently.
Exceptionally fluent reader 5	An avid and independent reader, who is making choices from a wide range of material. Able to appreciate nuances and subtleties in text.

INDEPENDENCE

RUNNING RECORD

INFORMAL ASSESSMENT

MISCUE ANALYSIS

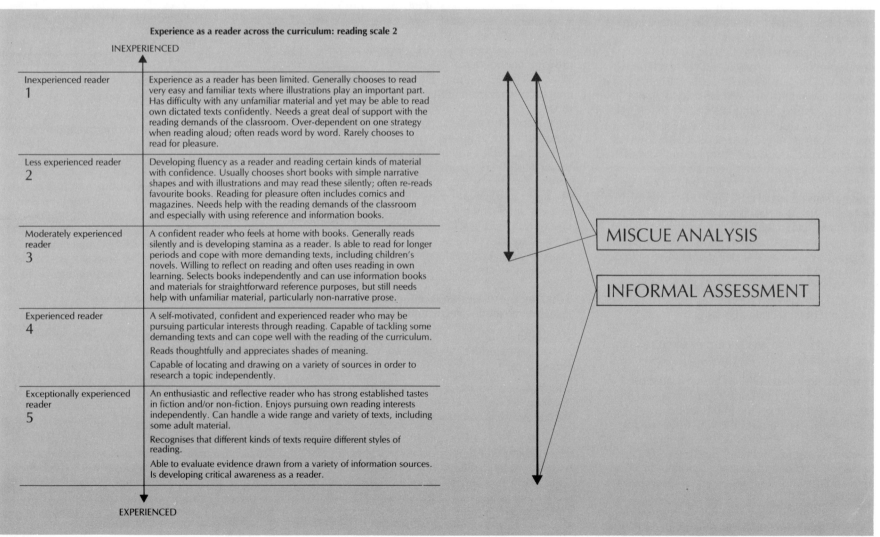

Experience as a reader across the curriculum: reading scale 2

INEXPERIENCED

Inexperienced reader 1	Experience as a reader has been limited. Generally chooses to read very easy and familiar texts where illustrations play an important part. Has difficulty with any unfamiliar material and yet may be able to read own dictated texts confidently. Needs a great deal of support with the reading demands of the classroom. Over-dependent on one strategy when reading aloud; often reads word by word. Rarely chooses to read for pleasure.
Less experienced reader 2	Developing fluency as a reader and reading certain kinds of material with confidence. Usually chooses short books with simple narrative shapes and with illustrations and may read these silently; often re-reads favourite books. Reading for pleasure often includes comics and magazines. Needs help with the reading demands of the classroom and especially with using reference and information books.
Moderately experienced reader 3	A confident reader who feels at home with books. Generally reads silently and is developing stamina as a reader. Is able to read for longer periods and cope with more demanding texts, including children's novels. Willing to reflect on reading and often uses reading in own learning. Selects books independently and can use information books and materials for straightforward reference purposes, but still needs help with unfamiliar material, particularly non-narrative prose.
Experienced reader 4	A self-motivated, confident and experienced reader who may be pursuing particular interests through reading. Capable of tackling some demanding texts and can cope well with the reading of the curriculum. Reads thoughtfully and appreciates shades of meaning. Capable of locating and drawing on a variety of sources in order to research a topic independently.
Exceptionally experienced reader 5	An enthusiastic and reflective reader who has strong established tastes in fiction and/or non-fiction. Enjoys pursuing own reading interests independently. Can handle a wide range and variety of texts, including some adult material. Recognises that different kinds of texts require different styles of reading. Able to evaluate evidence drawn from a variety of information sources. Is developing critical awareness as a reader.

EXPERIENCED

MISCUE ANALYSIS

INFORMAL ASSESSMENT

– drawing on previous experience to make sense of the book/text

Observing what the child knows about reading this book or this particular kind of book/text and about reading itself contributes to our understanding of the child's development as a reader. If the settings, language and social values are unfamiliar, it will be hard for the child to draw on previous experience in order to make sense of the text. Also racist and sexist messages in books will affect a child's reading. Therefore choice of book/text will play a crucial role in determining how a child reads it, how s/he feels about it and how much s/he understands.

– playing at reading

Young children often play-read, making up an elaborate and extended version of the story, often incorporating elements of other stories and of real events in their own lives. The book may be used as part of the 'reading' and the pages may be turned to accompany the story. It is not long before children begin to echo some of the intonation of the adult who has read to them, and will perhaps remember some memorable parts of the story (I'll huff and I'll puff. . .)

– using book language

When the child is having a go at reading a known book we can see clearly the language and experience they bring to construct the text and the degree to which they are taking on the author's voice. Book language is different from spoken language. One of the first things a child notices is the distinctive tunes of written language, e.g. 'In the light of the moon a little egg lay on a leaf.' Children often take on the 'tune' of a known book before they are able to read the words.

– reading the pictures

At the very early stages of reading it is likely that as a child becomes involved in play-reading, the pictures of a book become the focus for the interaction that takes place between a reader and the text – often the pictures *are* the text for a young child.

With growing knowledge and experience of stories and books and of how written language and written texts work, the child comes to know that it is the text that carries the story and that is read aloud, and that the words of the text do not change. Pictures then take on a shared role with the text in supporting the child's learning to read – turning the pages enables the reader to recreate the text.

focusing on print (directionality)

All writing systems work along two axes – horizontal and vertical. Children gradually work out that text in English, for instance, runs from left to right and top to bottom of the page. Questions such as, 'Can you show me where to start reading?' or 'Where do we go next?', and sometimes asking children to follow the print with their fingers, helps them to develop understanding of directional rules.

1:1 correspondence

Developing one-to-one correspondence is a significant pointer to reading progress, for the reader is matching the form s/he sees with the words s/he says. S/he is no longer recalling the message from memory but aiming to read the text itself. Predictions can now be checked against a number of language cues.

recognition of certain words

With experience children become aware that written language is made up of sequences of words. To recognise a sequence such as, 'Once upon a time' in context is an important step in a child's reading development; further development takes place when a child recognises each word of the sequence as having a separate identity. As a child starts to build up a repertoire of known words so s/he will begin to identify these words in a variety of contexts. Other words may be recognised for different reasons (e.g. because they are part of familiar environmental print). Gradually these words too will begin to be recognised when they appear in other contexts.

using semantic/syntactic/grapho-phonic cues

As the child becomes more experienced as a reader s/he will focus in more detail on the nature of written texts. In order to support a child's developing strategies and note a growing ability to draw upon language cues it is of obvious importance to identify the nature of the child's reading strategies so that positive support can be given.

when reading aloud

– does the child make use of the context to help work out the meaning (semantic cues), and does what s/he read make sense?
– does the child use knowledge of the structure of language (syntactic cues) to help work out meaning?
– does the child use knowledge of what words/letters look or sound like (grapho-phonic cues) to help work out an unknown word?

predicting

Making informed guesses and/or taking risks with print is a very important and integral part of learning to read. A child needs to know that these strategies are of positive assistance when reading and that s/he can have time to try out possibilities.

3 **Reading Samples** (reading in English and/or o	
This might include an element of silent reading	
Dates	Jan. '87.
Title of book/text (fiction or information)	'Drift' from the Blue Story House.
known text/unknown text	unknown
sampling procedure used: informal observation/running record/miscue analysis	informal assessment
1 **Overall impression of the child's reading:** • confidence and degree of independence • involvement in the book/text • the way in which the child read the text aloud	Read silently at great speed. Scanned text at first, made a good (not accurate) guess at what it was about.
2 **Strategies the child used when reading aloud:** • drawing on previous experience to make sense of the book/text ★ playing at reading ★ using book language ★ reading the pictures ★ focusing on print (directionality, 1:1 correspondence, recognition of certain words) • using semantic/syntactic/grapho-phonic cues • predicting • self-correcting • using several strategies or over-dependent on one	Clearly using every available cue including re-reading silently when aware of mistake. Several miscues she made she didn't correct, felt she didn't need to bother as she had got the sense of the text. Tries when tackling 'new' words to draw on previous knowledge of how words are put together. e.g. that-ches.
3 **Child's response to the book/text:** • personal response • critical response (understanding, evaluating, appreciating wider meanings)	Thought it was 'quite good, but a little difficult. Retold story very accurately very involved as if telling to audience. Remembered all characters.
4 **What this sample shows about the child's development as a reader.** **Experiences/support needed to further development.**	A competent reader who prefers to read silently. Re-reading if she thinks something doesn't make sense. Looking up meanings if she wants. Provide range of reading material.

★early indicators that the child is moving into reading

▲ T **1st year junior — girl**
Languages: **English**

The teacher chose this story for T. to read knowing that it was quite a complex text and wanting to discover how T. would respond to the challenge. It is obvious, on reflection, that T. has well-established strategies for getting at the meaning of what she reads.

This sample shows us in clear terms the kind of expectations a teacher can form of a reader's development as a direct result of this sampling procedure.

3 Reading Samples (reading in English and/or other community languages)

To include reading aloud and reading silently.

Dates	19.1.87.	4.3.87.
Title of book/text (fiction or information)	Mrs. Mopple's Washing Line	Each, Peach, Pear, Plum.
known text/unknown text	known text.	known text.
sampling procedure used: informal observation/running record/miscue analysis	informal assessment.	informal assessment.
1 **Overall impression of the child's reading:** • confidence and degree of independence • involvement in the book/text • the way in which the child read the text aloud	wanted me to begin Reading the page, then he completed	M. chose this book and said "I don't know it very well". I read the beginning of each page.
2 **Strategies the child used when reading aloud:** • drawing on previous experience to make sense of the book/text ★ playing at reading ★ using book language ★ reading the pictures ★ focusing on print (directionality, 1:1 correspondence, recognition of certain words) • using semantic/syntactic/grapho-phonic cues • predicting • self-correcting • using several strategies or over-dependent on one	Turning each page, looking carefully at print but not yet aware of directionality of print. Using picture cues. Self-Correcting - said, "No, no," when he turned 2 pages instead of one.	He supplied the endings eg. Tom Thumb, Pear Plum. Pointed out the people & said, "I know them" (eg. 3 Bears) "It's the story bears."
3 **Child's response to the book/text:** • personal response • critical response (understanding, evaluating, appreciating wider meanings)	"It's a story about her washing - I know this story". He read the book twice then picked up another book of the same size.	Read it again then said he didn't really like it!
4 **What this sample shows about the child's development as a reader.** **Experiences/support needed to further development.**	Draw attention to words and pictures. Show direction of print (L-R).	Increase confidence. More reading in one-to-one situations.

★early indicators that the child is moving into reading

These two samples help to highlight many aspects of M's early development as a reader in English. We are told how he feels about particular books, what he knows about how readers behave and how he participates in the shared activity of reading. There are also indications of the way in which the language of a book captures his interest, how he is building up a repertoire of familiar books and developing an ability to respond critically to what he reads.

There are a number of strategies a child can use to predict what might come next – picture cues, prior knowledge and experience of the type of text, knowing how written language works and how written language sounds – all these will help the child to read the next page, or phrase or word.

self-correcting

When a child begins to self-correct as s/he reads, s/he is making a very significant leap in reading development. S/he has come to realise that text must make sense, that written language is rule-based and that there exists a definite relationship between the way words look and the way words sound. In the light of this kind of knowledge the reader will confirm or reject an initial prediction.

using several strategies or over-dependent on one

Using a range of strategies which, by definition, involves a degree of risk-taking, is essential in learning to read. Many children who experience difficulty in learning to read are prevented from making substantial headway by the limited view they have of what is involved in becoming a reader. This view is often perpetuated where children are offered a combination of bland texts and a limited set of strategies with which to operate. (The sole set of strategies most commonly offered is one based on phonic analysis).

3 Child's response to the book/text

This section provides an opportunity to record children's comments and responses – either those that arise during the reading itself, or when discussion takes place afterwards. If the child chose this text it would be interesting to know why.

personal response

The quality of a child's response to a particular book/text will depend very much on the following factors:

  – who chose the book/text
    – whether or not the child found the text meaningful/enjoyable/worthwhile
    – whether the reader had time to browse, prepare and/or read silently before reading aloud
    – whether it was a known or unknown text

3 Reading Samples (reading in English and/or o

To include reading aloud and reading silently.

Dates	March 87
Title of book/text (fiction or information)	The Saga of Erik the Viking by Terry Jones
known text/unknown text	unknown
sampling procedure used: informal observation/running record/miscue analysis	informal assessment
1 **Overall impression of the child's reading:** • confidence and degree of independence • involvement in the book/text • the way in which the child read the text aloud	Completely engrossed in text and reading with obvious enjoyment. Read an extract fluently, accurately and with expression.
2 **Strategies the child used when reading aloud:** • drawing on previous experience to make sense of the book/text ★ playing at reading ★ using book language ★ reading the pictures ★ focusing on print (directionality, 1:1 correspondence, recognition of certain words) • using semantic/syntactic/grapho-phonic cues • predicting • self-correcting • using several strategies or over-dependent on one	Used a wide range of strategies, only hesitating over one or two words, e.g. fjord. Told me, before reading aloud, that he always takes note of the author when choosing a book but rarely notes an illustrator. In this case however he particularly enjoyed Michael Foreman's pictures and thought they played an important part in his enjoyment of the book.
3 **Child's response to the book/text:** • personal response • critical response (understanding, evaluating, appreciating wider meanings)	His eagerness to share his response to the text is an obvious indication of his enjoyment. Feels that this book is more sinister than the usual run of legendary stories and is enjoying that.
4 **What this sample shows about the child's development as a reader.** **Experiences/support needed to further development.**	Reading fluently with commitment and pleasure. Developing an awareness of authors' intentions. Shows a willingness to handle more complex texts. Encourage him to share his responses more often.

★early indicators that the child is moving into reading

▲ E *4th year junior — boy*
Languages: English

There are indications that E. is completely at home when reading this kind of narrative. Like many older pupils and adults he has built up a knowledge of books and authors that he particularly enjoys and is eager to discuss what he reads with others. He has a mature understanding of ways in which this writer (Terry Jones) can imply meanings that are not at first apparent.

critical response (understanding, evaluating, appreciating wider meanings)

Invite the child to talk about the reading. If you need to prompt them to say more, try to use open-ended questions that are supportive and encouraging. Younger readers in particular will want to tell you about the story or about the content in some detail and this will provide a picture of the child's understanding of the reading. While s/he is talking note also whether you think s/he has noticed details of the text, and recognised implied meanings – was s/he making comparisons with other reading, responding to the text as a reflective reader? Did what s/he said relate to what has been observed from the language and literacy conferences?

For children who are reading in languages other than English a monolingual English-speaking teacher will need to seek the support of bilingual colleagues/parents/or older children (if there is no bilingual development/community language teacher) to help in assessing children's development. If this is not possible the classroom teacher can find out a great deal by talking with the child in English about the reading. Reading in one language supports reading in another so all strategies noted contribute to the picture of the child's progress in biliteracy.

4 What the sample shows about the child's development as a reader

This section is for commenting on any changes and developments that have taken place since the previous sampling. Observations might include the following considerations:

– whether the child is able to handle more complex texts, or is more able to persist with a challenging text
– evidence of greater interactions with and growing interest in texts
– evidence of increased confidence and sense of control
– developing ability to monitor own reading and to self-correct. Developing ability to predict confidently and to use cues, especially context cues
– increasing interest in a range of texts, and a growing appetite for reading
– evidence of reading for learning across areas of the curriculum

Experiences/support needed to further development

It will be helpful to record a summary of plans that were made for and with the child in relation to future reading experiences. These might include:

– suggestions for further reading (supported and unsupported, in English and other community languages)
– ways of enabling the child to share her/his reading with others (adults and peers)
– suggestions for ways in which the child can write about her/his reading, in some form of reading log or journal

Sampling reading: some practical considerations

(a) Becoming familiar with formal sampling procedures such as Running Records and Miscue Analysis may be time-consuming at first. However, teachers adapt and simplify the procedures and become quick at doing them. Many teachers believe that, once familiar with the techniques, they never listen to children read in quite the same way again and find themselves applying the thinking behind Running Records and Miscue Analysis to their informal sampling. Consequently they find themselves needing to do fewer formal sampling procedures with children and spending more of their time on quicker informal assessments.

(b) Sampling a child's reading in depth can give a teacher a great deal of information about that child – far more than can be gleaned from several shorter sessions with a child. Analysis helps observation by, for example:

– revealing more about how a child is self-correcting and behaving when s/he meets difficulties and therefore more about how s/he can be helped, for example by not 'jumping' in and correcting a child who is reading aloud, by encouraging a child to 'rerun' a sentence.
– revealing more about the suitability of the reading material and the child's understanding and enjoyment of what s/he is reading. Many teachers find this particularly useful for their more fluent readers; they can discuss with them what they have read silently and point them towards other suitable, perhaps more challenging, material.

Consequently teachers may find themselves spending only a little more time listening to children read overall, but learning correspondingly much more about their children's reading.

4 Writing samples

This section of the observation and sample sheet is intended to be a framework for reviewing a child's writing development regularly. It can be done once a term or more frequently, and the sheet can be copied and incorporated into a teacher's day-to day record system. The writing sample section provides a structured way of looking in depth at particular pieces of writing.

Many schools already collect examples of children's writing in folders which become cumulative records. This method of sampling draws on that practice and allows for the systematic collection and analysis of work.

Writing Samples: notes on the headings

Writing in English and/or other community languages

Most children will be writing in English but some bilingual children will also be literate in another language and if they are encouraged to do so, they may be using their community language for some of their school writing. If teachers do not read this language they will have to rely on the child, or on bilingual colleagues or parents for help with translation. Children's writing in their first or community language may in some cases be more developed and more confident than their writing in English and it will be of great value to obtain a full picture of them as writers by including examples of all their writing in these samples. It will be interesting to note in what sort of contexts children choose to write in their community language. When sampling bilingual children's English writing it will be important to note how long they have been learning English.

'Writing' to include children's earliest attempts at writing

In order that these records may be of use with the very youngest children this sample form is designed to allow you to record observations of children's earliest development as writers, and should be applicable to their earliest attempts at writing and their writing-cum-drawings. Some children may at this stage be communicating much more through their pictures than they are through their texts.

Often a child's commentary on her/his own writing can reveal a great deal lying behind apparently simple symbols. 'I want it to say, "Two boys tripped over a rock"', said a child who had written letters from his name under a drawing.

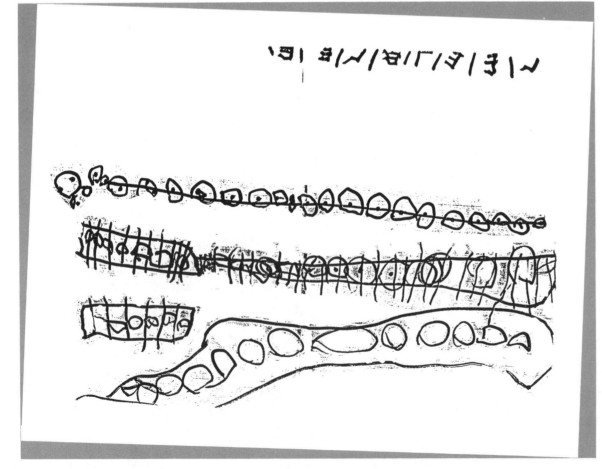

4 Writing Samples (writing in English and/or oth...)
'Writing' to include children's earliest attempts at writing

Dates	12.2
1 **Context and background information about the writing:** • how the writing arose • now the child went about the writing • whether the child was writing alone or with others • whether the writing was discussed with anyone while the child was working on it • kind of writing (e.g. list, letter, story, poem, personal writing, information writing) • complete piece of work or extract?	Came to do a drawing - white paper and felt tips of different sizes. Talking whilst drawing "That's a ladder" "This is a man up the ladder" "He's painting the house"
2 **Child's own response to the writing.**	"This is how my name look"
3 **Teacher's response:** • to the content of the writing • to the child's ability to handle this particular kind of writing • overall impression	More confident about this writing. Talks along while drawing and writing.
4 **Development of spelling and conventions of writing.**	Small capital letters along top of paper - alternating 3 letters, E, L, I
5 **What this writing shows about the child's development as a writer:** • how it fits into the range of the child's previous writing • experience/support needed to further development	Needs encouragement to write a little larger. He is writing his name repeatedly but most of the 'story' is connected with the drawing at the moment

Please keep the writing with the sample sheet

◄▲ 	L 	*Nursery — boy*
Languages: **English**

This writing sample records a typical occasion when the child is drawing and writing. The teacher appreciates the role of the child's commentary in the whole process. At this stage it is hard to separate out writing from drawing and talking, although L's preoccupations with writing his own name is noted.

1 Context and background information about the writing

Any piece of writing is a product of a particular context; this section underlines the importance of considering context in some detail when you are analysing a writing sample. It gives an opportunity to notice:

- how the writing arose (you may like to record whether the topic was self-chosen, what the curriculum context was, whether the writing was a response to something recently read).
- how the child went about the writing (how absorbed the child was in the writing, how long they worked on it, whether they wrote more than one version).
- whether the child was writing alone or with others (it may have been a collaborative piece of work, or other children may have been involved in editing).
- whether the writing was discussed with anyone while the child was working on it (it may be helpful to record the level of support being given by teachers to other adults, or children, or to look at the way the child responded to suggestions).
- what kind of writing it is — children may be writing in a way close to speech, a personal 'expressive' voice, or may be taking on voices from their reading (traditional stories, adventure comics, advertisements or

information books). 'Poetic' kinds of writing (poem, story) may be earlier to develop than 'transactional' writing (reports, arguments). Generally they will find *narrative* writing (whether it is fictional or a real-life narrative) easier to manage than *non-narrative*. This space allows you to define the 'voice' you find in the writing or to say what form is being used.

- whether the writing is a complete piece of work or an extract? (You may have chosen to sample a complete short piece of writing or to look at one chapter from a story in chapters, for example. By the same token, you may be sampling an early draft of a piece of writing which is going to be worked on further, or a final draft – it may sometimes be interesting to compare the two.)

2 Child's own response to the writing

This section is a chance to record children's own comments on their writing, made either in the course of the writing or afterwards with the teacher. If children don't volunteer a comment, you can obviously invite them to say what they think.

Children may want to tell you more about the writing, or they may be able to evaluate what they have done and say how pleased they are with their work. Does it do what they set out to do? Which parts are they most satisfied with?

4 Writing Samples (writing in English and/or o[ther])
'Writing' to include children's earliest attempts at writing

Dates	
1 Context and background information about the writing: • how the writing arose • how the child went about the writing • whether the child was writing alone or with others • whether the writing was discussed with anyone while the child was working on it • kind of writing (e.g. list, letter, story, poem, personal writing, information writing) • complete piece of work/extract	M. wrote this retelling after listening to the story on a story tape several times. Probably particularly interested in it because of the Caribbean stories told by storytellers who visited recently. Wrote the complete book in one go – took a whole morning. First draft.
2 Child's own response to the writing.	Very pleased with it. He has talked a lot about the story since listening to the tape.
3 Teacher's response: • to the content of the writing • to the child's ability to handle this particular kind of writing • overall impression	I was delighted. It's a very faithful retelling, retelling much detail and language. It's also a lengthy narrative for him to have copied with alone.
4 Development of spelling and conventions of writing.	He has made excellent attempts at several un-familiar words which he has only heard, not read, before. Apart from vowels in the middle of words he is getting close to standard spelling.
5 What this writing shows about the child's development as a writer: • how it fits into the range of the child's previous writing • experience/support needed to further development	It is the longest thing he's done and the best in technical terms. He is happy with re-telling and likes to have this support for his writing, but it would be nice to see him branching out with a story that is not a retelling soon.

Please keep the writing with the sample sheet

◀▲ M *Middle-infant — boy*
Languages: **English**.

This sample shows a child writing a really extended text for someone of his age, supported by the fact that it is a retelling of a traditional story. The teacher notes the significance of this in his development as a writer.

One day anansi met hare
and they went to a
tree fooll of food
anansi
sing
soi[...]

1st Draft, original spelling

One day anansi met hare and they went to a tree fooll of food
anansi had tosing a little soing to get the rope and the rope
did Not come dawn its self his mother dropt it dawn and he
climb up it he towld hare not to tell but at ferst he did not
tall but in a little wille he did.

He towlld eliphont and the tottos and the poqupin and the caml
and they saing the little soing and dawn came the rope and they
all clambd on it and the rope swuing rawnd and rawnd.

and they all screemd and thir screemds wock Anansi up and he
shawtdid to his mother it is not Anansi but robbers cut the rope.

and she cut the rope and the anmls fell and the elephent flatnd
his fas and the totos crct his shell and the caml brocka bon in
his humpe and pocupin brock all his pricls.

3 Teacher's response

An opportunity to evaluate this particular piece of writing and to say how far it seems to succeed in its own terms. Is the *content* interesting? What about the *kind of writing* – is the child using this form confidently? And finally, how does this piece strike you as a reader – what is your reaction to it?

4 Development of spelling and conventions of writing

Spelling

It will be helpful in this section to look analytically at the child's spellings and to note any particular patterns of error (such as a tendency to reverse letters in the middle of words), and any positive signs of progress. What does this piece of work show about a very young child's understanding of the writing system? If a child is 'inventing spellings' are these spellings good guesses? What does the writing show about the child's visual awareness of spelling and knowledge of common letter combinations? Are there any obvious points that could be worked on?

Written language conventions

What do you notice from this piece of writing about the child's awareness of how to present written language, lay out different kinds of texts, and punctuate written language for the reader? As the child develops as a writer, how far is s/he able to mark sentences or paragraphs, and observe other conventions of written language (e.g. inverted commas)?

5 What this writing shows about the child's development as a writer

Do you feel there have been any important changes since the last time you completed a writing sample with this child?

Some growth points you might be noticing are:
- increasing interest in writing and readiness to write
- increasing confidence and sense of control as a writer
- increasing ability to persist and work at more extended texts
- increasing ability to consider a reader's needs, and to 'write like a reader'
- increasing ability to look back over own writing and identify points which need changing, expanding, or correcting

4 Writing Samples (writing in English and/or other community languages)

'Writing' to include children's earliest attempts at writing

Dates	February '87	
1 Context and background information about the writing: • how the writing arose • how the child went about the writing • whether the child was writing alone or with others • whether the writing was discussed with anyone while the child was working on it • kind of writing (e.g. list, letter, story, poem, personal writing, information writing) • complete piece of work or extract?	Class teacher – English version. Following work about stories – A fairy story/folk tale 'with a difference'. Wrote English version almost entirely by herself – though it was preceded by a lot of general talk about stories and their conventions.	Community language teacher. Bengali version. I suggested doing a Bengali translation of the story and she was very enthusiastic. Made it into a book. Did most of the translation herself, needs help in selecting a few words in Bengali.
2 Child's own response to the writing.	Didn't say much but very committed to this piece of work.	
3 Teacher's response: • to the content of the writing • to the child's ability to handle this particular kind of writing • overall impression	Delighted with it! Narrative – excellent grasp of narrative style: very good sequence. Delightful original touches – 'strawberries and popcorn'. Detail in pictures adds to story.	Suggested the translation to reach a wider audience. A good piece of translation in Bengali. Has shown quite a lot of confidence in looking for appropriate words. Quite a lot of Sylheti words used rather than standard Bengali.
4 Development of spelling and conventions of writing.	Basically 'canopt' the English spelling system now – occasional slips e.g. where/were. Uses basic punctuation; use of speech marks still a bit inconsistent.	Few spelling mistakes.
5 What this writing shows about the child's development as a writer: • how it fits into the range of the child's previous writing • experience/support needed to further development	She particularly enjoys long illustrated narratives but she's also written a number of descriptive pieces and explanations! Has the ability to match style/type to content. She's very confident and can draw constructively on her reading and knowledge of book language. Work on punctuation.	First attempt at this kind of writing, she's shown enthusiasm and confidence. Discussion about standard Bengali words would be useful. Could help development by reading more Bengali books.

Please keep the writing with the sample sheet

Once there was a little girl called
Little Red Riding Hood. One day
she wanted to go to her grand
ma's house. So she set off
through the woods but she forgot
the way and got lost.

এক ছিল এক ব্লের্ট মেয়ে তার নাম ছিল
রেড রাইডিং হুড। এক দিন এ তার নানির
বাড়ি যাছিলো। জেন রাথজতু পরিছয়ে ঘেললা।

Then she saw a beautiful woman with
really long hair and the woman said
"who are you?" and little Red Riding Hood said
"I'm Red Riding Hood" and who are you?"
The woman said "I'm Rapunzel" Then
Rapunzel said "why are you crying?" and RRH
said "I've lost my way to my grandma's house.

এ একটি সুনদর মেয়েলুকের দেখা ঘলা।
মেয়েলুকাটি তখন বলল তুমি কে?। রেড রাইডিং
হুড বলল অপমপর নাম রেড রাইডিং হুড।কিন্তু
তুমি কে? মেয়েলুকাটি বলল অপমপর নাম
রেথপনজেলা। রেথপনজেল বলল তুমি কেন কান্দন
রেড রাইডিং হুড বলল অপমি এপরথর নানির
বাড়ি যাছিলাপম কিন্তু রাথজতু পরিছয়ে
ঘেলনিছি।

Then Rapunzel said The Three
little pigs might know your grandma's house. So Rapunzel took RRH
to the third little pig's house
which was made of bricks.

তখন রেথপনজেল বলল তিনি ছোটা শুকুর
শুকুর হুকপর নানির বাড়ি জিনতত যপরবো।
তপর যর রেথপনর রেথপনজেল রেড রাইডিং
হুডকে তিন নপরমকর শুকুরের অথিতত নিয়ঁ
ঘেলা।

◀ ▲ ☐S ☐ *4th year junior — girl*
*Languages: **Sylheti, Bengali, English***

*This sample shows what can be learnt about a child's
competence as a writer when a class teacher can work closely
with a bilingual development/community language teacher.
The story reveals a sophisticated awareness of narrative style
and an ability to play with story structure.*

How it fits into the range of the child's previous writing

This box also offers an opportunity to take stock of the child's range as a writer in English and/or other languages and to see whether this piece is representative of the kind of writing s/he does, or whether it marks a new development of some kind. It may be possible to relate this writing to other pieces the child has done in the same genre, to identify possible influences on the writing — for instance a particular text the child has read — or to note in this piece a feature not previously evident in the child's writing (a style s/he is trying out, a kind of writing not previously attempted, self-correction of a particular point).

Sampling writing: some practical considerations

(a) Many teachers are well aware of the value of going through a piece of first draft writing with a child correcting and editing it together and if appropriate deciding on what to do with the writing. Often this will take only a few minutes but sometimes teachers take the opportunity to discuss an aspect of the writing in more depth (e.g. looking at spelling patterns, discussing the use of dialogue, or finding out more about the child's attitude towards, and enjoyment of,

writing). Inevitably a writing discussion (or 'conference') of this kind with a child will take more time and a teacher will perhaps only be able to do a few a week. However, as with doing reading samples, teachers find the benefits of such discussions to the child and themselves are enormous.

Jotting down notes about a child's writing, with the child, in the writing sample section can become a natural 'extension' to such discussions.

It can be decided with the child if a piece of writing is a representative sample, important enough to be dated and kept (or photocopied) when finished to become a record of the child's development. This can be, for example, writing done totally independently, writing that has been re-worked or writing done with support and collaboration. The sample form will provide a record of the context of the writing.

(b) To help organisation for 'writing samples' teachers have found it useful to have:
– tick-off charts to ensure that samples are done with all children
– writing folders — where children keep all their first draft pieces of writing and things they are currently working on
– a box in the classroom where children can put first draft writing they need help with or want to edit with the teacher.

```
DISABLED


I feel imprisoned in this life
trapped, different and .... embarrassed
I hate the way people stare at me,
mostly little kids
Treating you like you're not human.
Then you get people who pity you.
Asking if they can do stupid things
they know you can do.
I wish they would treat you normally.
I'm just the same as them, in my brain
but my body doesn't work.
Yet they treat me as if I'm more
different than that.
I want to get up and scream "look I'm
just like you".
Sometimes when I see other people
running I want to cry.
```

4 Writing Samples (writing in English and/or oth

'Writing' to include children's earliest attempts at writing

Dates	Boy 4th Year 12.2.87
1 Context and background information about the writing: • how the writing arose • how the child went about the writing • whether the child was writing alone or with others • whether the writing was discussed with anyone while the child was working on it • kind of writing (e.g. list, letter, story, poem, personal writing, information writing) • complete piece of work or extract?	Project on Transport T. was considering the problems the disabled might have with transport. Wrote 1st draft without support. We discussed an episode of 'Grange Hill' which had illuminated the problems/feelings of the disabled for him.
2 Child's own response to the writing.	T. felt able to empathise with the disabled. He thought he was successful in conveying this in his writing.
3 Teacher's response: • to the content of the writing • to the child's ability to handle this particular kind of writing • overall impression	His use of language/ structure encourages an empathetic response. Blank verse- confuses the personal and third person.
4 Development of spelling and conventions of writing.	One spelling corrected- confident speller. Well aware of the format necessary for this type of writing. Able to use punctuation to strengthen a point.
5 What this writing shows about the child's development as a writer: • how it fits into the range of the child's previous writing • experience/support needed to further development	Writes for a wide variety of purposes. Is pleased with his ability to convey moods and feelings. Richness of the vocabulary used in all his writing reflects his level of reading. Needs to develop critical awareness through conferencing and expose him to the way poets structure their work for effect.

Please keep the writing with the sample sheet

 ◀ ▲ T **4th year junior — boy**
Languages: **English**

In the notes on this sample, the teacher responds first of all to the writer's intention — to explore the difficulties sometimes experienced by the physically disabled — and observes the confidence apparent in his use of his chosen form, his vocabulary, and his attention to punctuation — all of which suggest that he would now be able to benefit from looking more analytically at the way poems are made.

Appendix A
Organisation and storage of the PLR

The Primary Language Record and the Observation and sample sheet are both hole-punched and can be stored in ring-binders. However other types of storage have been used successfully by teachers and it is hoped that teachers will use the record flexibly in ways that will suit their needs and their methods of classroom organisation.

Confidentiality

All of the staff who teach a child and the child's parents should be able to have access to the Primary Language Record itself. But it must be remembered that, as an official record, the PLR is a confidential document and when not in use should be stored in a secure place such as a filing cabinet, a locked cupboard, or the school office. The accompanying observation and sample sheet is, of course, not confidential and can be kept in any convenient and accessible part of the classroom or work area.

Using the observations and sample sheets in the classroom

Easy access

The observations and sample sheets are meant to be used as part of teachers' own records, and are designed to be used for jotting down notes. Easy access to them is therefore important, both for the class teacher and for any support teacher/staff who might want to add to the record.

Some teachers have concerns about making notes on children's work when the children are in front of them. However, in classrooms where the record is being used, right from the start with the language and literacy conference the child is actively involved in her/his own development. Children soon come to understand that they can be positively involved in evaluating their own progress, and enjoy the time they have with the teacher when a reading sample or a writing sample is being done.

Organising observation

Some teachers organise class activities in a way that allows them to focus on a particular child/children and a particular aspect of language, for example:

— observing children read or write (either individually or as part of a small group), or

— children talking/discussing together in pairs/groups

A teacher can have the relevant 'diary of observations' sections at hand to note observations as s/he visits different individuals or groups.

Similarly, when a child reads a book with their teacher or discusses a piece of writing with their teacher, notes can be made in the samples section (parts 3 and 4) and any relevant information such as a photocopy of the child's writing or the actual running record/miscue analysis can be attached to the sample section or stored with it.

Storage

When choosing a method of storage many teachers have felt the following to be important considerations:

a) Note-taking in the classroom, with children, should be made as easy as possible.
b) It should be easy for children to find their own records (or folder containing them).

Using a ring-binder

Some teachers prefer storing the PLR and the observation and sample sheet in a single ring-binder.

Pieces of writing accompanying the writing samples, and running records or miscue analyses accompanying the reading samples can be: stapled or clipped to the back of the observation and sample sheet; hole-punched and stored in the ring-binder; or kept in a hole-punched plastic wallet or envelope in the ring-binder.

The buff record forms can be stored separately in another ring-binder or, when they are not being used, can be kept in a box-file or in the individual children's manilla folders in the school office.

Using a 'concertina' file

Some teachers may prefer the 'ease of access' of a 'concertina' file. This method may make it more possible for a child to find their own sample sheet or file away a chosen piece of writing. As mentioned before, the PLR should be stored separately.

Plastic wallets or envelopes for each child can be slotted appropriately into the concertina file for storing relevant pieces of work, notes on a reading assessment, etc.

Using individual folders for each child

Many teachers prefer children to have their own folders. Any pieces of work referred to in the observation and sample sheet can be photocopied and stored in the folder.

All the folders can be kept together in a box, a filing cabinet, etc. This form of storage also allows plenty of room for collecting any other relevant notes, pieces of work, or lists of books read by the child, which some teachers like to keep together to give an overall picture of the child's development.

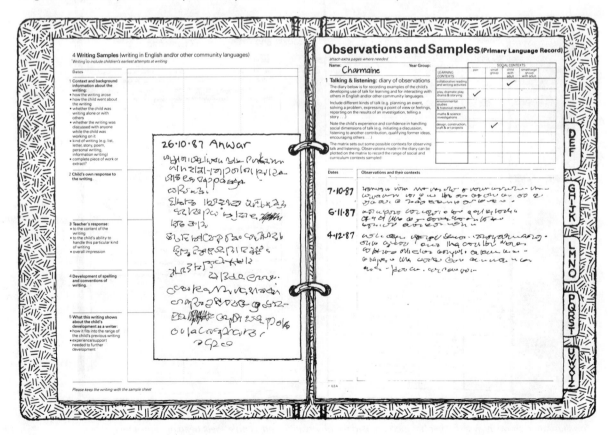

The child can be involved in this process and can decide with the teacher which pieces of work to select.

This method of storage makes it very easy for even very young children to find their own folders for the teacher.

Storing parts of the observation and sample sheets separately

Although some teachers value having all aspects of langugage recorded together so that a whole picture of the child is built up and cross-referencing is made easier, there are others who prefer a more flexible method of organisation. Similarly, some schools may have decided to use only one or two aspects of the observations and sample sheet.

By photocopying any of the four different sections of the observation and sample sheet, one or more sections could be stored separately in different ways in different parts of the classroom.

1. For example, the reading samples sections could be kept all together in the book corner to be at hand when a teacher hears a child read.

2. The writing sample sections might be stored separately in individual folders/wallets for each child with the accompanying pieces of writing.

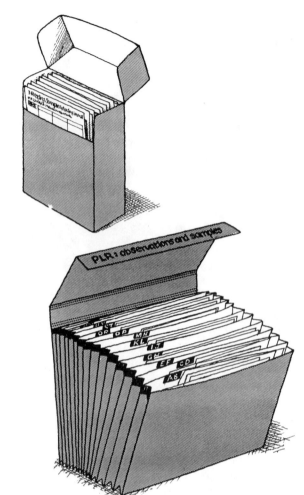

Many teachers like to keep a writing folder, selecting with the child pieces of aided and unaided, first or final draft writing over the year, to go in it.

3. Some teachers like to keep the talking and listening observation sheet all together in a very accessible part of the classroom so a quick entry can be made there and then when the situation arises (e.g. on a clip board).

Finally, some schools have cut up the observation and sample sheet and used the headings as part of their day-to-day recording systems. This gives the opportunity to make a much fuller record of development and is just as useful when completing Part B of the Primary Language Record.

Completed observation and sample sheets

If a child's observation and sample sheet is filled up during the year another sheet can be started. Completed observation and sample sheets can be stored with the PLR, or kept together with the new observation and sample sheets so that it is easier to make reference to a child's progress.

If you run out of space in certain sections on the observation and sample sheet you can photocopy that section and attach it as an 'add-on' sheet. Or, if the sheets are used with a ring-binder, new sheets can be hole-punched and added.

Keeping a log/tick-off chart

Some teachers designed their own tick-off charts for their class so that they can see at a glance which part of the PLR or of the observation and sample sheet they have made entries on for each child. Some felt this helped to focus on a particular child or children.

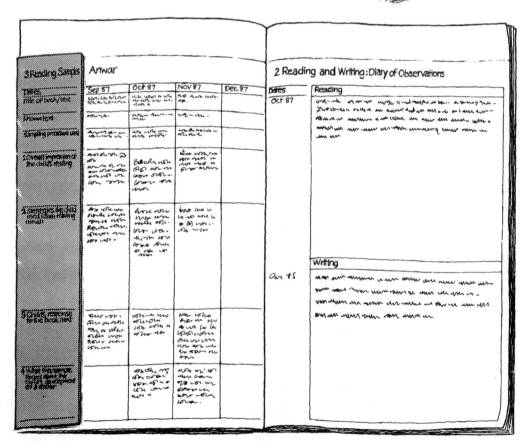

This illustration shows how a teacher has incorporated the observation and sample sheet headings into a record book.

	main record			observations			samples	
	child conference/parent discussion A	B	C	Talking and Listening	Reading	Writing	Reading	Writing
Anwar	✓ ✓			✓	✓	✓	✓	✓
Charmaine	✓ ✓				✓		✓	✓
Claire	✓			✓	✓	✓	✓	
Costas	✓ ✓			✓			✓	✓
Delon	✓ ✓				✓	✓	✓	
Farah	✓ ✓			✓	✓	✓	✓	✓
Farida	✓			✓	✓		✓	✓
Hafsa	✓ ✓				✓	✓	✓	✓

Appendix B
The languages bilingual children understand, speak, read and write

The language-using experience of many bilingual children may be wide and diverse. Throughout the PLR Handbook we have introduced the terms currently used to describe languages other than English that children may use and know: home language, community language, and 'first' language.

These terms may not always accurately reflect the complexity of use of any one child and are often used as a shorthand for describing a complex area. For example, at home (for 'home' language) one or more languages as well as English may be spoken. A child's 'first' language may be a language other than English spoken by two parents; it may be the language spoken by one parent; it may be English; two languages may have been acquired together and neither could be called 'first'.

The diagram below shows examples of some children's knowledge of a language (or languages) other than, or as well as, English.

Androulla understands Greek but does not use it at home. Kofi understands Yoruba but does not speak, read or write it – English is spoken at home with his parents, and older brothers and sisters. Josie attends the synagogue and is learning to read and write Hebrew. Iqbal speaks Sylheti at home with his family, and is learning to read and write Bengali; he also attends the Mosque school and is learning to read the Qu'ran in Arabic. Concetta goes to the Italian community school; she understands, reads and writes Italian, and *can* speak it but at the moment prefers not to. Juliana first went to school in Portugal before coming to live in England and speaks, reads and writes Portuguese. Essra's family is Turkish-speaking but use English in talking with her. Krishna's mother is Italian and her father Bengali; conversations between them at home are in English, but when relatives and friends come to visit, all three languages may be spoken.

In recording the languages understood, spoken, read and written by children it will be important to consult their parent(s) and to be guided by what they say about their children's knowledge and use of home/community languages.

One of the results of living on an island such as Britain is that the *monolingual* experience of the majority of the population is seen to be 'normal', when in fact for most people in the world the *multilingual* experience – both personally and in society – is the norm, and people expect to be able to use more than one language. Bilingual children reflect the normality of the multilingual experience outside Britain, and many will have wide linguistic backgrounds.

Some of the general factors which have contributed to this breadth are these:

– population movements and patterns of migration over the last 100 years – people have moved (and are moving) away from countries of origin, and have settled (or are settling) in countries which have offered opportunities for work, and as people move they have added the language(s) of the country of settlement to their linguistic repertoire. For example, Indian families, whose first language is Gujerati, settled in East Africa, and learned Swahili (and other languages) and subsequently settled in Britain – many forced to flee from Uganda.

– the language of literacy may not be the language spoken and used at home – *for example,* the language/dialect Sylheti is spoken, but its speakers read and write in Bengali; Panjabi-speaking families whose country of origin was Pakistan will write in Urdu, the first language of Pakistan.

– children may have access to a third language of literacy for religious purposes – *for example* Muslim children learning to read and write in Arabic for studying and learning the Qu'ran – in addition to using a home/community language other than English.

– the languages used at home, or known by a family may reflect the complex language situations in the parents' countries of origin *for example,* where several languages will be used by most of the population as in Mauritius.

	Knowledge of languages *in addition to English*			
	understands	can speak	can read	can write
Androulla	Greek	Greek	–	–
Concetta	Italian	Italian	Italian	Italian
Essra	Turkish	–		
Kofi	Yoruba	–	–	–
Iqbal	Sylheti	Sylheti	Bengali and Arabic	Bengali
Josie	–	–	Hebrew	Hebrew
Juliana	Portuguese	Portuguese	Portuguese	Portuguese
Krishna	Bengali and Italian	–	–	–

Appendix C
Informal assessment

A teacher is informally assessing a child's growth and development in reading whenever s/he:

- becomes aware of the influence of a particular story/book on a child's dramatic play or on their writing

- shares a book with a child/group of children

- listens to a child read aloud

- discusses a child's response to a book

- observes a child browsing and/or sharing books (fiction and non-fiction) with others

- notes instances when a child chooses to read silently, for the first time/for sustained periods

- initiates reading conferences where a child talks generally about her/himself as a reader or more particularly about the quantity, range and variety of books read

- notices ways in which a child uses reading for learning across the curriculum

- sees evidence of a bilingual child using knowledge of reading in Turkish, for example, to support learning to read in English

These and many more examples generally inform our understanding of how and what children are learning. For bilingual children reading in English, the length of time they have been learning English will also be significant.

For the purposes of *this* informal assessment however, which forms part of the reading sample, it will be useful to have a clear procedure, and also to have particular points in mind when observing a child's reading.

An informal assessment focuses on a child reading a particular text. It is a form of assessment that can be used with children of any age from three to eleven, and the elements in the child's reading which the teacher will be noticing will obviously depend to some extent on the age of the child and on her/his experience as a reader. For sampling reading, an informal assessment may prove to be particularly useful:

- with very young or inexperienced readers who have not yet realised that the text carries the message

- with much older and more experienced readers, who generally choose to read silently, and whose reading is largely free of miscues

The informal assessment is as applicable to reading in home/community languages as to reading in English, though monolingual teachers may have to seek the help of bilingual development/community language teachers or other speakers of the child's first language in order to obtain a full picture of their reading in that language.

Suggested procedure

1 A relaxed atmosphere

Children will feel more at ease and will perform better as readers if they are in a supportive situation. Some factors which may help to create a relaxed atmosphere are:

a) The child may choose the text.

This may be a book they know already, are currently reading or a text that is unfamiliar. It may be in English or another language. It may be from a story book or a book of information. The important point is that it should be a text that the child *wants* to read.

b) The child may preview the text with the teacher.

This is particularly useful when the text is one that is not known to the child. The teacher and the child look through the text together, predicting what kind of a text it might be, using title, blurb, illustrations.

c) The child may read silently (if s/he is able).

The age at which a child moves into reading silently varies widely and will depend on the range of her/his reading experiences and maturity as a reader.

In silent reading a child is able to make better use of available language cues. S/he can read at a self-chosen pace, having the time to scan the text as s/he searches for meaning. S/he can question the author's intention, reflect on what has been read without the constraints of reading phrase by phrase aloud. Silent reading is the most common and effective type of reading used by adults so it is important that children are encouraged from the beginning to spend time browsing among books where they can pay attention to meanings evident in illustrations, rehearse texts, reflect on possibilities and probabilities in story and in print, as this early reading behaviour is a rehearsal prior to being able to read silently.

d) The child may practise a section before reading it aloud.

Children find it very difficult to read a text aloud 'cold' – and so do adults! It will be useful if they are specifically encouraged to practise before they read part of the text aloud.

e) The teacher and the child discuss the text.

Discussion forms an integral part of an informal assessment. Teachers can learn a great deal from the quality of a child's response to a text in discussion.

2 The informal assessment process

During the assessment teachers will be using the headings of the reading sample sheet to help them to structure their observation of the child's reading.

They will therefore focus on the three main aspects of the reading highlighted in the headings:

- overall impression

- strategies the child used when reading aloud

- child's response to the book/text.

In the 'strategies' section teachers will not have a formal system of marking miscues to refer to (as in a Running Record or a Miscue Analysis) but will nevertheless be noting the way the child uses all the cues present in the text, and will be observing the child's behaviour as a reader (attention to pictures, pausing, re-reading, etc.)

This simple procedure should enable teachers to structure the time given to the reading sample effectively, and provide a helpful framework for observation.

Informal assessment: bilingual development/community language teachers and bilingual children

Many schools have bilingual development/community language teachers on the staff and these teachers will obviously play a very important role in assessing a bilingual child's reading development in a language other than English. They will be able to contribute to the child's Record and to the all-round picture of a child's growth in biliteracy.

If there is no support in a school then an English-speaking monolingual teacher can discover much that is valuable about a child's reading in another language through discussion and listening to the child reading aloud. It is also crucial that the class teacher values the child's linguistic and cultural experiences in and outside school and appreciates how learning in one language facilitates learning in another.

Some of the things to look for when listening to a child reading in a language that is unfamiliar to you could be: the child's pleasure and enjoyment in reading, her/his degree of involvement in discussing the text during and after reading, the confidence with which s/he chose the book and subsequently the way s/he read it aloud.

Appendix D
Running record

Before describing the procedure it is important to see it in the context of listening to children read aloud which is part and parcel of everyday classroom practice.

Reading aloud is a way in which a child can share her/his enjoyment of stories and books with an adult. It can also be a means whereby a teacher can monitor a child's development as a reader, at the same time helping the child to establish positive strategies for learning. With the latter points in mind it is useful to think of a Running Record as a way of looking more closely at what a young child is thinking and doing as s/he reads; to analyse the miscues and so make plans on how best to take the child forward.

At the very early stages a child will be retelling the story, using the pictures as cues, remembering parts of the language of the book, finding the tune on the page and generally making the story their own. The reading of the book may well be accompanied by questions and comments, as the child continues to refine understandings. Soon s/he will come to realise that it is the text that carries the message.

With experience the reader will become aware of:

- directional rules

- one-to-one correspondence

- a number of words

- the patterns of written language

and will be hypothesising about grapho-phonic associations.

With further experience s/he will be focusing more closely on the text itself, and applying self-correcting strategies to confirm or reject predictions. A Running Record is a simple but effective way of observing how a child handles text and of discovering how s/he is developing as a reader on a move from dependence to independence. (Refer to Reading Scale 1 on page 26.)

Procedure

1 Select a book which is familiar (known) to the child and make a choice about the way the miscues are to be recorded.

2 Either make a copy of the text, or part of the text, and mark the miscues on it

OR

record the miscues on a blank sheet of paper, keeping to the same linear arrangement as the text of the book

OR

adopt the system shown in the diagram on the left using the markings in the key.

Analysis

It was Marie M. Clay who devised the *Running Record* and further details of it can be found in *The Early Detection of Reading Difficulties* (Third Edition, 1985). In the following extract from her book she discusses and explains ways in which a child might respond when reading a text aloud and provides support for the teacher in posing the kinds of questions that need to be asked as the 'errors' are noted.

'What cues does he depend on?

- *Does the child use meaning? If what he reads makes sense, even though it is inaccurate, then he is probably applying his oral language knowledge to his reading.*

- *Is what he says grammatical? If it is, his oral language is influencing his responding. If it is not, there may be two reasons. Perhaps his personal 'grammar' does not contain the structures used in his reading book. Or, if he is paying close attention to detail, or to word by word reading, he may not be allowing his control over English syntax to influence his choices.*

- *Does he use visual cues from the letters and words?*

- *Does he read word by word as if recalling each word from a memory bank, unrelated to what has gone before? He may not realise that reading is like speaking, and that his*

Title: 'Spot's First Walk' by Eric Hill

Text	Running Record	Child's Comments
Off you go, Spot!	/ / / /	He's speeding off
Don't get lost.	/ / /	
Not in there,	Now / Not(SC) / /	I don't think that says 'now' – it doesn't make sense.
Spot.	/	
Hello!	/	
What's in the	/ / /	
hutch,	hut / hutch	The first time I was going to the hut, I didn't want to go because I thought the pigeons was there.
Spot?	/	
Have a	/ /	
nice day	/ /	
That's a	That's T /	What did that say?
funny noise …	/ /	
(tap, tap etc.)		That's Woody Woodpecker.
and that's	/ /	
a nice smell.	/ / /	
Thank you	/ /	
Are you hungry,	/ / hiding / hungry	I don't think that's right (when asked why, he replied – 'because it would have "ing" there, my mum told me')
Spot?		
Look in	/ /	
the flower	/ /	
bed	/	
What have	/ /	
you found?	/ /	
Now for a drink …	/ / / /	
Don't	/	
fall in	/ /	
Poor Spot!	Poor T /	
Time to go	/ / /	
home.	/	
Sally	/	
Spot	/	
What have you	/ / /	
been doing	/ /	
Spot?	/	
Not a lot.	/ / /	

☐ words in boxes are under 'flaps' in text

A A stroke (/) indicates a word read correctly.
B A substitute word is written above the word in the text
C An omission is marked with a circle.
D A word given is marked T for TOLD.
E A self-correction is marked thus:
    e.g. Are you hiding/hungry(SC)

---

language behaviour is a rich source of help in choosing correct reading responses.

To work out whether the child is responding to the different kinds of cues that could be used you need to look at every error that the child makes and ask yourself "Now what made him say that?" "Did he miss out on the visual cues?" "Was he ignoring meaning?" It is misleading if you do this selectively; you must analyse every error and count those that show this, or that kind of cue. You want to be able to conclude, on sound evidence, that "he pays more attention to visual cues than to meaning", or "he is guided by structure and meaning but does not search for visual cues".

It is only when you go to the trouble of analysing all the errors that you really get any indication of what his strategies are on reading.

When teachers are familiar with taking running records they may want to write M for meaning, S for structure and V for visual cues on the record form and to record, by circling, which cues the child was using. Notice that what you are recording in this case is your best guess: you cannot know what cues the child used. A record may show one, two or three types of cues used on any one error. If you write M S V alongside each error or self-correction and circle the cues you think the child used, the uncircled letters will then show the cues neglected.

Consider the error first. What cues up to that error was the child using? Think only of the information the child had before the error occurred. Then consider the self-correction. What extra information did the child use in the self-correction?

Cross-checking strategies

Can the child check one kind of information with another? Can he get movement and language occurring together in a linked or coordinated way? Does he check on language prediction by looking at some letters? Can he hear the sounds in a word and check whether the expected letters are there? A child with outstanding memory for what he hears or with very fast language production often has difficulty in slowing up enough to enable him to learn the visual discriminations. Yet good readers search for cues from different sources which confirm a response.

Self-correction

Observe and enter in the running record any self-correction behaviour. The child discovers cues that tell him something is wrong. He is aware that a particular message is to be communicated and tries to discover this by using cues. Efficient self-correction behaviour is an important skill in good reading.'

In this next section a child's Running Record has been analysed by the teacher and it is interesting to see how this record plays a crucial role, alongside other sections of the PLR, in K's development as a reader in English and Bengali.

Example of a Running Record, illustrating how this procedure contributes to a developing picture of a reader

K, a speaker of Sylheti and English, is learning to read and write in Bengali and English. He is 6 years old and in a top infant class. He has lived in England for about four years and has enjoyed a range of traditional stories and rhymes from Bangladesh (at home), and from many other countries (at school).

The book he has chosen to read with the teacher has an imitative rhythmic quality and the language is patterned in such a way as to lead the child on from one page to the next. How a child comes to understand this book will depend very much on circumstances. How much experience has s/he had of 'reading' cumulative stories and rhymes that come from a variety of different social and cultural settings? K's experiences had prepared him well for taking on this book.

The school's head teacher explains that it is the school's policy to value children's knowledge of the traditional stories and rhymes that they bring with them to school, and in K's case this experience was rooted in the cultural heritage of Bangladesh. At school, children are also introduced to other stories and rhymes and

children's story repertoires are consequently rich and varied.

There are a number of comments that the class teacher made about this Running Record that are helpful in assessing growth and development, for example

Known text/unknown text
'known a little bit, heard once last term.'

Child's response to the book/text
'full of comment as always, even before book opened, but then K. derives enjoyment from everything'

"so many times the Each Peach Pear Plum bit" (referring to number of title pages).

"They are having such a good time when they eat that pie because the baby and everyone is smiling" and "I wish I could be Robin Hood, but I don't drink beer because it's not good for you".

Strategies the child used
Attention to print: many words known. Used initial/sense/picture when unknown, and occasionally gave up and asked.

Overall impression of the child's reading
Absolutely laden with comments (couldn't write such a flood down).

K enjoyed it and tackled it well, using a good range of cues.

About right for him (more than 90% with ease – probably about 95%)

Title 'Each Peach Pear Plum' by Janet and Allan Ahlberg	Name K.	DoB	Date 8.1.87
TEXT	Child's Comments	TEXT	Child's Comments
Each Peach Pear Plum / I spy Tom Thumb	So many times the Each peach pear plum part (refers to titles)	Jack and Jill in the ditch / I spy the Wicked Witch	
Tom Thumb in the cupboard s. table' / I spy Mother Hubbard		Wicked Witch over the wind wood / I spy Robin Hood	the wicked witch s/c by going back
Mother Hubbard down the stairs cellar / I spy Cinderella		Robin Hood in his den the din? / I spy the Bears again	s/c den ✓
Cinderella on the in stairs / I spy the Three Bears	s/c three the	Three Bears still hunting / THEY spy Baby Bunting	
Three Bears out hunting / I spy Baby Bunting		Baby Bunting safe and dry smile / I spy Plum Pie	porridge or pie pie!
Baby Bunting fast asleep / I spy Bo-Peep		Plum Pie in the sun stairs / I spy . . .	
Bo-Peep up the hill / I spy Jack and Jill	"I don't know what it's called" (Pointing to well!)	. . . EVERYONE	

Appendix E
Miscue Analysis

What this sample shows . . .
It shows a clear progress from last term.
Is self-correcting effectively at times. Uses
print primarily.

To extend our understanding of K's
experience with books, with stories and with
other readers there is one more piece of valuable
information gathered from the Primary Language
Record – the language and literacy conference,
that the teacher recorded in the Autumn Term.

'Likes reading by himself, and at school with
teacher, and with J. (sister). Has some Bengali
books at home. Likes the chapter books at story
time, especially Ursula Bear, and Peter Pan
"because it was exciting: some happy things and
some poor things." He chose to read *Are You My
Mother* and read it confidently. Says "I can read
very well, I think." Says that reading and writing
are his best things. His sister tells him stories out
of her brain in Bengali, and his father reads him
letters from his grandmother in Bangladesh. His
brother tells him stories of videos – Indian films.
Wishes he had his own book of the Hobyahs.'

Introduction

'Miscue Analysis' is a procedure for analysing
what children do as they read a text aloud, based
on the work of Kenneth and Yetta Goodman in
the U.S. during the late 1960s.

Since then it has been adapted and
modified by others, including Helen Arnold, and
Cliff Moon. The procedure described here is a
further adaptation, drawing on the sources
mentioned.

Miscue Analysis involves the observation,
recording and evaluation of 'mistakes' or 'errors' a
child makes or appears to make when reading
aloud. The term 'miscue' is applied as it suggests
that the reader is processing the text using
successful strategies and/or those which may be
inappropriate to the understanding of what is on
the page.

Using Miscue Analysis

This procedure can be used when a child is a
Moderately fluent/Fluent reader on Reading Scale
1 ('Becoming a reader') — for example, one who
chooses to read silently but often needs support in
reading unknown texts.

It can also be used with children on Reading
Scale 2 ('Scale of experience') who are
Inexperienced, Less experienced or Moderately
experienced readers.

The strategies used when reading can be
identified and appropriate support provided to
help a child develop as a confident, fluent and
independent reader.

Preparation

Selecting the text

In selecting a text for Miscue Analysis it is
important to consider the child's linguistic and
cultural experience and to choose material that is
likely to be of interest and provide an enjoyable
reading experience for the child. The text should
be one of sufficient quality to support the child's
reading of it, for example, it should read aloud
with a natural flow. This will minimise the
chances that the child's difficulties are because of
the text.

The selected text should not be well known
to the child and should be one that makes
demands of the reader without causing
frustration. (As a rule of thumb, if there is more
than one miscue in ten words then the child is
reading at frustration level and is unlikely to gain
sufficient meaning from the text to make it
worthwhile.) It is best to have several texts
available so that if the child has great difficulty, or
reads one text too easily, another text can be
used.

Selecting the passage

From a book or text, choose a passage for the
child to read aloud of about 150-300 words and
make a copy. (This should not be too near the
beginning in order that the child has time to get
into the text.) The copy is then used by the
teacher for marking miscues during the session
(or following the session if the procedure is to be
tape-recorded). It is often a good idea to
tape-record the child reading the passage aloud,
particularly at first when a teacher is learning to
listen for miscues and to use the coding symbols.
There may also be other occasions when it is
useful to tape-record, for example when there is
particular concern about a child and analysis
needs to be particularly detailed.

Whenever possible, the child should read
from the original book/text so that the reader has
the opportunity to make full use of the context
cues available.

Procedure

In this particular adaptation an element of silent
reading has been included as part of the
procedure and in addition to a Miscue Analysis.
This will offer children an opportunity to
demonstrate their growing ability to read silently
as well as read aloud even if they are still
operating at the very early stages of silent reading
(sub-vocalising). It will also convey to children
that the ultimate aim in learning to read is to be
able to do so silently, where pace and enjoyment
are in the control of the reader. This sense of
control means that they can organise the ways in
which they come to understand texts without
being over-concerned about the element of
performance in reading aloud.

The procedure adopted for Miscue Analysis
is divided into four parts:

1 Read the text silently.
2 Retell or describe the text.
3 Read the text aloud.
4 Discuss the text in more detail with the
teacher.

It is important that the child understands
what is involved in the four parts of the procedure
in advance – so that s/he has a clear picture of the
whole activity.

1 Read the text silently

Ask the child to spend time in reading the text for
her/himself. The amount of time given will
depend very much on the experience and age of
the reader.

During this time the child's strategies can be
observed and noted, for example, how far was
s/he able to sustain reading silently or did s/he

choose to read aloud to her/himself? It will also be valuable to note the child's degree of confidence and involvement while reading.

2 Retell or describe the text

The teacher might say to the child: 'I would like you to tell me the story', or 'I would like you to tell me what it was about'. This process of retelling clearly demonstrates comprehension as a direct result of reading silently. It must be remembered, however, that the skill of retelling or recalling requires practice and some children will have had less practice than others. Bilingual children who are not fluent in speaking or reading English may need encouragement and perhaps more time to make meanings explicit.

3 Read the text aloud

The child is then asked to read the text aloud. The teacher might say, 'I would like you to read this aloud to me as well as you can. I want to see how well you can manage without my helping you. Just try to keep the reading going. If you really get stuck I will help you.'

As the child reads, or when listening to the recordings of the reading, mark the miscues on the duplicate copy as shown in the example.

The purpose of this part of the procedure is to reveal what a reader does when encountering a difficulty in the text. When the teacher is aware of the strategies a child is using s/he is able to plan appropriate support, encouraging the child to use positive strategies which enable her/him to make sense of the text, for example:

– reading on, in order to help work out a word

– going back and repeating a previously read sentence/section, in order to establish or check the context

– stopping if what is read does not make sense and correcting the miscue

– using the grapho-phonic features of words to check guesses

– using more than one strategy to guess the word, for example, syntactic and semantic cues.

4 Discuss the text in more detail with the teacher

If the text is a story let the child talk about one or two of the characters, the story setting and aspects of the plot. The more experienced the reader the more able s/he will be to talk about the implicit meanings and/or ambiguities that might exist in a complex text.

If the text is an information text, for example, and describes a process, the child could be discussing the process in some detail, adding any relevant background information, and/or demonstrating an understanding of what kind of text it is and the purpose it serves.

An analysis of one miscue sample

R. is a third year junior child whose first language is English.

The Tortoises' Picnic

There were once three tortoises — a father, a mother, and a baby. And one spring day they decided that they would like to go for a picnic. They picked the place they would go to, a nice wood at some distance off, and they began to get their stuff together. They got tins of salmon and tins of tongue, and sandwiches, and orange squash, and everything they could think of. In about three months they were ready, and they set out, carrying their baskets.

They walked and walked and walked, and time went on, and after about eighteen months they sat down and had a rest. But they knew just where they wanted to go and they were about halfway to it, so they set out again. And in three

years they reached the picnic place. They unpacked their baskets and spread out the cloth, and arranged the food on it and it looked lovely. Then Mother Tortoise began to look into the picnic baskets. She turned them all upside down, and shook them, but they were all empty, and at last she said, 'We've forgotten the tin opener!' They looked at each other, and at last Father and Mother said, 'Baby, you'll have to go back for it.' 'What!' said the baby, 'me! Go back all that long way!' 'Nothing for it,' said Father Tortoise, 'we can't start without a tin-opener. We'll wait for you.' 'Well, do you swear, do you promise faithfully,' said the baby, 'that you won't touch a thing till I come back?' 'Yes, we promise faithfully,' they said, and Baby plodded away, and after a while he was lost to sight among the bushes.

And Father and Mother waited. They waited and waited and waited, and a whole year went by, and

they began to get rather hungry. But they'd promised, so they waited. And another year went by, and another, and they got really hungry. 'Don't you think we could have just one sandwich each?' said Mother Tortoise. 'He'd never know the difference.' 'No', said Father Tortoise, 'we promised. We must wait till he comes back.'

So they waited and another year passed, and another, and they got ravenous. T

'It's six years now,' said Mother Tortoise. 'He ought to be back by now.'

'Yes, I suppose he ought,' said Father Tortoise. 'Let's just have one sandwich while we're waiting.'

They picked up the sandwiches, but just as they were going to eat them, a little voice said, 'Aha! I knew you'd cheat.' And Baby Tortoise popped his head out of a bush. 'It's a good thing I didn't start for that tin-opener,' he said.

KATHERINE BRIGGS

62

The coding symbols: a marking key

① substitution
— the word substituted is written above the corresponding word in the text.

e.g. *When*
Then Mother Tortoise began to look into the picnic baskets.

② self-correction
— the miscue is written above the word in the text and is marked as shown.

e.g. They picked up the sandwiches, but *c/they* just as they were going to eat them, a little voice said, 'Aha! I knew you'd cheat.'

③ repetition
— the words repeated are underlined. Double underlining indicates words have been repeated twice.

e.g. 'It's six years now,' said <u>Mother Tortoise</u> 'He ought to be back by now.'

④ omission
— the word is circled in the text.

e.g. So they waited, (and) another year passed, and another, and they got ravenous.

⑤ insertion
— the inserted word is written above an insertion mark.

e.g. And in ^*the* three years they reached the picnic place.

⑥ reversal
— (there is no example of this in the marked text shown but) the words reversed are marked with a continuous line.

e.g. 'yes, I suppose he ought,' said|Father

⑦ hesitation
— an oblique stroke is marked before the word paused at,

e.g. 'Well, do/you/swear, do you promise faithfully,' said the baby, 'that you won't touch a thing till I come back?

⑧ long pause, teacher gives help
— oblique stroke as in ⑦. Mark the word given by the teacher with a T.

e.g. So they waited and another year passed, and another, and they got /ravenous. T

(numbers refer to those in the marked text)

Analysis

In analysing the miscues marked on the page, it is important to look at the balance of positive and negative strategies the child has used in reading the text aloud.

''Positive'' strategies e.g. intelligent substitutions are signs that a child is reading for meaning and is understanding the general sense of the text. ''Negative'' strategies are those which hinder the child's general understanding of the text and which show that s/he is not reading mainly for meaning (e.g. omission of important words without self-corrections, over-reliance on grapho-phonic cues).

Throughout the reading R. demonstrated her ability to use several strategies in attempting a word, relying on grapho-phonic cues only when others didn't help her, as in 'tongue' (tun-guoo), and showing that this can often be misleading.

R. read the text confidently and with the expectation that it should make sense. In the discussion of the story that followed, she needed support from the teachers in remembering the story and recognising the underlying meanings, such as the baby tortoise not setting out for the tin-opener at all.

To support R's reading of a text, she might be invited to think about particular aspects of the story whilst she is reading, or told beforehand that she will be asked afterwards to say what it is about. She could be encouraged to read with a partner, to retell stories or to discuss a taped story within a small group. During a class-story more opportunities might be made to talk about the subtleties and nuances of meaning in a text so that R. learns to consider more deeply what she is reading.

The grid shows the balance of miscues for the marked text illustrated.

Type of miscue	Substitition	Self-correction	Omission	Insertion	Reversal	Long pause	Total
positive	12	8	7	4	—	—	31
negative	7	—	5	—	—	1	13

(Hesitations and repetitions are not included in the grid as they show styles of reading rather than strategies.

3 Reading Samples (reading in English and/or ot
To include reading aloud and reading silently.

Dates	23 · 3 · 87
Title of book/text (fiction or information)	Tortoise's Picnic by Katherine Briggs
known text/unknown text	unknown
sampling procedure used: informal observation/running record/miscue analysis	miscue analysis

1 Overall impression of the child's reading:
- confidence and degree of independence
- involvement in the book/text
- the way in which the child read the text aloud

· reading very confidently
· performing as to an audience
· trying to make the text flow (perhaps to the detriment of her understanding?)

2 Strategies the child used when reading aloud:
- drawing on previous experience to make sense of the book/text
★ playing at reading
★ using book language
★ reading the pictures
★ focusing on print (directionality, 1:1 correspondence, recognition of certain words)
- using semantic/syntactic/grapho-phonic cues
- predicting
- self-correcting
- using several strategies or over-dependent on one

· text is probably about right, she made quite a lot of miscues but mostly positive
· self-corrected by predicting & trying to make sense of the text.
· uses a good balance of cues
· obviously drawing on her wide experience of story language when reading this

3 Child's response to the book/text:
- personal response
- critical response (understanding, evaluating, appreciating wider meanings)

· she was amused by this story—with some prompting.
· understood the twist at the end (but only after talking it through).

4 What this sample shows about the child's development as a reader.

Experiences/support needed to further development.

· conscious of R performing when reading aloud & perhaps not focusing on the overall meaning
· positive, confident attitude to reading
· needs to discuss more what she has read
· assessing her reading at her silently may be useful in future.

★ early indicators that the child is moving into reading

References

Children's authors and books referred to in the text

Verna Aardema
Bringing the Rain to Kapiti Plain
Illustrated by Beatriz Vidal
Macmillan, 1981

Janet and Allan Ahlberg
Each Peach Pear Plum
Kestrel Books, 1978

Funnybones
Heinemann, 1980

The Jolly Postman
Heinemann, 1986

Peepo!
Kestrel Books, 1981

Betsy Bang
The Old Woman and the Rice Thief
Illustrated by Molly Garrett Bang
Hamish Hamilton, 1978

Stan and Jan Berenstain
Bears in the Night
Collins, 1971

James Berry
A Thief in the Village and other stories
Hamish Hamilton, 1987

Katherine Briggs
Tortoises' Picnic *in*
The Blue Storyhouse
edited by David Jackson and Dennis Pepper
Oxford University Press, 1976

Ruth Brown
A Dark Dark Tale
Andersen Press, 1981

John Burningham
Mr. Gumpy's Outing
Cape, 1970

Eric Carle
The Very Hungry Caterpillar
Hamish Hamilton, 1970

P D Eastman
Are You My Mother?
Collins 1962

Michael Ende
The Never Ending Story
Penguin Books, 1984

Gail Haley
A Story, a Story
Methuen, 1972

Eric Hill
Spot's First Walk
Heinemann, 1981

Ted Hughes
The Iron Man
Faber & Faber, 1968

Pat Hutchins
Rosie's Walk
Bodley Head, 1970

David McKee
Not Now, Bernard
Andersen Press, 1980

Robert N Munsch
The Paper Bag Princess
Hippo Books, 1982

Hiawyn Oram
Angry Arthur
Illustrated by Satoshi Kitamura
Andersen Press, 1982

Catherine Sefton
The Ghost Child
Illustrated by Charlotte Voake
Heinemann, 1984

Maurice Sendak
Where the Wild Things Are
Bodley Head, 1967

Simon Stern
The Hobyahs
Methuen, 1977

and
Betsy Byars
Paula Fox
Rosa Guy
Dick King-Smith
Margaret Mahy
Michael Rosen

Teachers' books referred to in the text

Helen Arnold
Listening to Children Reading
Hodder & Stoughton, 1982

Douglas Barnes & Frankie Todd
Communication and Learning in Small Groups
Routledge & Kegan Paul, 1977

Douglas Barnes
Language the Learner and the School
3rd edition
Penguin Books, 1986

Marie M Clay
The Early Detection of Reading Difficulties
3rd edition
Heinemann, 1985

Department of Education & Science
A Language for Life
(The Bullock Report)
H.M.S.O., 1974

Kenneth S Goodman
Language and Literacy: the selected writings of Kenneth S Goodman
edited by Frederick V Gollasch
2 Volumes
Routledge & Kegan Paul, 1982

Kenneth S Goodman, *editor*
Miscue Analysis: Applications to Reading Instruction
Urbana, Illinois: ERIC/N.C.T.E., 1973

M A K Halliday
Learning How to Mean: Explorations in the Development of Language
E Arnold, 1975

Inner London Education Authority
Improving Primary Schools
(The Thomas Report), 1985

The Junior School Project:
a summary of the Main Report 1986

Inner London Education Authority
Research & statistics Branch
Catalogue of Languages Spoken by ILEA School Pupils
RS1055/86
June, 1986

Kenneth Katz
Languages of the World
Revised edition
Routledge & Kegan Paul, 1986

William Labov
Language in the Inner City: Studies in the Black English Vernacular
Philadelphia: University of Pennsylvania Press, 1972

David Mackay, Brian Thompson & Pamela Schaub
Breakthrough to Literacy
Schools Council Programme in Linguistics and English Teaching
Longman for the Schools Council, 1970

Margaret Meek
Learning to Read
Bodley Head, 1982

Cliff Moon
"Making Use of Miscues when Children Read Aloud" *in*
Children Reading to Their Teachers
National Association for the Teaching of English, 1984

Margaret L Peters
Spelling: Caught or Taught? A New Look
Routledge & Kegan Paul, 1985

Frank Smith
Reading
2nd edition
Cambridge University Press, 1985

Writing and the Writer
Heinemann Educational, 1985

Michael Stubbs, *editor*
The Other Languages of England: Linguistic Minorities Project
Routledge & Kegan Paul, 1985

Lev S Vygotsky
Mind in Society: the Development of Higher Psychological Processes
Cambridge, Mass: Harvard University Press, 1978

Constance Weaver
Psycholinguistics and Reading: From Process to Practice
Cambridge, Massachusetts: Winthorp Publishers, 1980

Gordon Wells
Language Learning and Education
NFER/Nelson, 1985

We would like to thank:

Ventura Publishing Ltd., for permission to reproduce the text of **Spot's First Walk** by Eric Hill (copyright Eric Hill 1981) first published by William Heinemann Ltd.

Penguin Books Ltd. for permission to reproduce the text of **Each Peach Pear Plum** by Janet and Allan Ahlberg, Kestrel, 1978.

Associated Book Publishing (U.K.) Ltd. for permission to reproduce **The Tortoises' Picnic** from **Dictionary of British Folk Tales** by Katherine Briggs, Routledge & Kegan Paul, 1971.